1

Little Known Tales That Boggle Your Mind

They are stranger Than fiction

Alton Pryor

Little Known Tales That Boggle Your Mind

They are stranger Than fiction

ISBN: 978-0-692-34898-7

LCCN: 9780692348987

Alton Pryor

Stagecoach Publishing
5360 Campcreek Loop
Roseville, CA 95747
stagecoach@surewest.net
www.stagecoachpublishing.com

I like the dreams of the future better than the history of the past.
  Thomas Jefferson

Life is a gift to be used every day,
Not to be smothered and hidden away;
It isn't a thing to be stored in the chest
Where you gather your keepsakes and treasure your
best;
It isn't a joy to be sipped now and then
And promptly put back in a dark place again.

Life is a gift that the humblest may boast of
And one that the humblest may well make the most
of.
Get out and live it each hour of the day,
Wear it and use it as much as you may;
Don't keep it in niches and corners and grooves,
You'll find that in service its beauty improves.
            Edgar A. Guest

Table of Contents

1

Charles Lindbergh
The Rogue Aviator

Charles Lindbergh in flight gear.

C harles A. Lindbergh started his flying career as a barnstorming daredevil, walking on the wings of flying aircraft and performing parachute stunts.

Lindbergh was born February 4, 1902. He spent most of his childhood in Little Falls, Minnesota. His father was an attorney, and a later on, a congressman.

Lindbergh seemed born to fly. At age 10, his mother took him to several air races. He became hooked on flying.

He entered the engineering program at the University of Wisconsin and failed the course. He dropped out and later enrolled in the Army Air Service Cadet Program in San Antonio, Texas, where he finished first in his class.

Lindbergh became the chief pilot on a new air mail route between St. Louis and Chicago. This was a new service and was dangerous. Thirty one of the first forty pilots hired to fly the mail routes perished in crashes.

Charles ate up the challenge. He later wrote, "The best way to cope with danger is to keep in contact with it."

When Lindbergh heard that New York hotelman Raymond Orteig was offering $25,000 for the first pilot to fly non-stop across the Atlantic, he set his sights on the prize.

Lindbergh found backers to provide the $15,000 needed to construct the plane to make the transatlantic flight. The plane was dubbed, "The Spirit of St. Louis" in honor of the contributors who supplied the money to build it.

Lindbergh traveled by train to San Diego to meet with Donald Hall at Ryan Airlines. Lindbergh and Hall had a lot in common. They both attended flight school in Austin, Texas. Hall was 28 years old and Lindbergh was 25.

Lindbergh's Spirit of St. Louis in which he flew non-stop from New York to Paris.

Hall designed the plane Lindbergh would fly under the direct supervision of Lindbergh. It was a highly modified version of a conventional Ryan M-2 strut-braced monoplane, powered by a Wright J-5C engine.

Hall's design maximized the plane for fuel capacity. There were no co-pilot accommodations, nor room even for a radio or a parachute. The fuel tanks were located in front of the cockpit.

While flying, Lindbergh was not able to see directly ahead. He used a periscope mounted on the left side of the plane to see forward of the aircraft.

The Spirit of St. Louis is considered one of the most famous aircraft ever built. The plane has been enshrined at the Smithsonian Institution's National Air and Space Museum alongside the Wright Brothers aircraft.

To fund his project, Lindbergh organized a presentation for a number of St. Louis businessmen. He hoped they would see his vision for commercial aviation.

He decided to show his financial backers how a non-stop flight between America and Europe could demonstrate the possibilities of aircraft. He was aware, too, that what he was doing would place St. Louis in the foreground of commercial aviation.

The first to pledge money to the project was Major Albert Bond Lambert. He pledged $1,000 toward the flight. He committed the amount only after Lindbergh himself pledged $2,000 of his own savings toward the venture.

By February of 1927, Lindbergh received full funding. The investors included Harold M. Bixby, Harry F. Knight, Harry H. Knight, Albert Bond Lambert, J.D. Wooster Lambert, E. Lansing Ray, Frank H. Robertson, William B. Robertson, and Earl C. Thompson.

The group became known as the "St. Louis Backers"

When Lindbergh met with the plane's designer, Don Hall, he knew they had only two months to complete it to meet the guidelines of the contest. It was a formidable task and even Lindbergh sometimes held doubts of its possibility.

After he discussed plans for the aircraft with Ryan's chief engineer Donald Hall, Charles became convinced that the deadline could be met. He placed an order for the monoplane on February 25, 1927.

Ryan Aircraft Chief Engineer Donald Hall works on plans for the famed "Spirit of St. Louis" aircraft

Hall and Lindbergh agreed on most issues regarding the plane's design. On other points, they compromised.

Since the fuel tanks would be in front of the pilot, Hall was concerned about forward visibility. Both Hall and Lindbergh knew what the tragic result would be if a single fuel line should rupture. There was also the question of pilot fatigue.

Hall decided that a total new design was a better option than modifying an older Ryan M-2. He didn't feel the Ryan M-2 model could make the 3,600 mile trip between New York and Paris with ample fuel reserve.

The dedicated designer worked 36 hours straight at one point to meet the deadline. He logged 90-hour-weeks to reach the 60-day goal.

During those 60-days of design work, Lindbergh, too, was kept busy. He taught himself the fine art of aeronautical ocean navigation which was new and unproven.

Lindbergh used sailing charts and "gnomonic" maps. A gnomonic map projects displays of great circles as straight lines. Thus, the shortest route between two locations in reality corresponds to that on the map.

He planned every detail of his trip and evaluated the necessity of every item he would carry. For instance, he chose to leave his parachute behind so he could carry more fuel. Likewise, he passed on taking a radio.

Lindbergh's fuel-saving concerns reached the point where he even trimmed the edges off his maps. He removed unnecessary pages from his notebook and declined to take along night-flying equipment. He became fanatical about saving weight on the plane.

When the plane's design neared completion, Lindbergh applied to the National Aeronautic Association as a contestant for the Orteig prize. He was regarded as a long shot.

Other contestants used multi-engine planes with multiple pilots. Lindbergh was the only contestant to fly alone, and in a single-engine plane.

There was a single-engine Bellanca entered in the race, but it too would carry multiple pilots. Some called Lindbergh the *Flying Fool* despite his vast aircraft experience.

Lindbergh standing by his plane in 1927.

Lindbergh waited for favorable weather to begin his flight. He arrived on Long Island on May 12, 1927.

When pressed by reporters about discarding his radio for the flight, Lindbergh said, "When the weather is bad, you can't make contact with the ground. When the weather isn't bad, a pilot doesn't need a radio.

The question of his eligibility to compete for the Orteig prize came into question. The rules stipulated that 60 days must elapse between acceptance of his papers and take-off of the flight.

His St. Louis backers told him to fly when he was ready, despite the prize.

It was a misty Friday morning on May 20, 1927, when Lindbergh rode from his Garden City hotel and rode to Curtiss Field to prepare for takeoff. He had gotten little sleep the night before.

Even at the early hour, 5,000 onlookers were on hand to see his takeoff. The takeoff concerned him, as he had a mere 5,000 feet to lift off the ground and gain enough altitude to clear the trees and telephone wires at the end of the airfield.

The Spirit of St. Louis had never been tested carrying 425 gallons of fuel, plus the 25 gallons of extra fuel Lindbergh ordered when he found the tanks built for the plane came out oversize by 25 gallons.

A bucket brigade was formed to fill the plane's five fuel tanks. By 7:30 a.m., the tanks were filled to the brim, causing the wheels of the plane to sink into the muddy ground.

At last, Lindbergh and his Spirit of St. Louis rumbled down the runway in New York. The plane weighed 5,250 pounds, of which 2,750 pounds was fuel.

Despite many uncertainties, Charles readied himself for takeoff. At 7:51 a.m., he buckled his safety belt, stuffed cotton in his ears, and strapped on his helmet. At 7:52 a.m., he took off for the long solo flight to Paris.

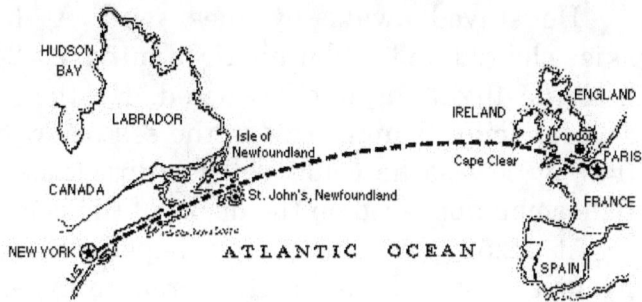

Map Provided by: www.charleslindbergh.com

Lindbergh's flight plan from New York to Paris.

With him, he carried five sandwiches, water, his charts and maps and a limited number of other items. The heavily-loaded plane went splashing and bouncing down the muddy runway.

As the load shifted from the wheels to the wings, Charles had less than 2,000 feet of runway left to get into the air. The telephone lines at the end of the airfield were coming up fast.

With less than 1,000 feet of runway left, Lindbergh lifted the plane sharply, clearing the wires by 20-feet. He was airborne at last.

As Lindbergh flew over Cape Cod and Nova Scotia, ice formed on the plane as he attempted to pass through the clouds. The lack of sleep the night before was telling on him, even though he was less than six hours into his flight.

In order to keep his mind alert, Lindbergh flew only 10 feet above the ocean. As night fell, the sea was obscured by fog. At 7:52 p.m., twelve hours after his takeoff, he climbed to 7,500 feet to stay above the rising cloud cover.

He stayed awake by sheer will. At last, the skies cleared and so did his tired mind. At 24-hours into the flight, he felt less tired. He then noticed several small fishing craft in the sea below him. He flew by low so he could yell for directions, but no fishermen appeared on the decks of the boats.

At 12:52 p.m., Lindbergh hoped to reach the French coast in daylight. He increased his air speed to 110 mph. At last, the English coast appeared. This brought him wide awake.

His log book showed that at 2:52 p.m., the Spirit of St. Louis was over the French coastal town of Cherbourg. He had only 200 miles to go to reach his destination in Paris.

At 5:52 p.m., he touched down at the Le Bourget Aerodrome, Paris, France. It had taken him 33 hours, 30 minutes, 29.8 seconds to complete the journey.

"I saw the lights of Paris a little before 10 p.m. (5 p.m. New York time). A few minutes later, I was circling the Eiffel Tower at an altitude of four thousand feet."

A crowd of 100,000 people swarmed around the plane, hoisting the pilot on their shoulders and cheering. The newspapers dubbed him, *The Lone Eagle* and *Lucky Lindy*.

The kidnapping of his 20-month old son, Charles Augustus Lindbergh, Jr., was a devastating event in Lindbergh's life. It occurred March 1, 1932. The child was taken from his nursery on the second floor of the Lindbergh home.

It was at 10 p.m. the child's nurse informed the Lindbergh's that their son was missing. A ransom note demanding $50,000 for the child's return was found. Investigators found traces of mud on the floor of the nursery.

Two sections of a ladder were used to reach the second story nursery window. One of the sections was split or broken where it joined the other. There were no blood stains or fingerprints in or about the nursery.

A copy of the Lindbergh ransom note.

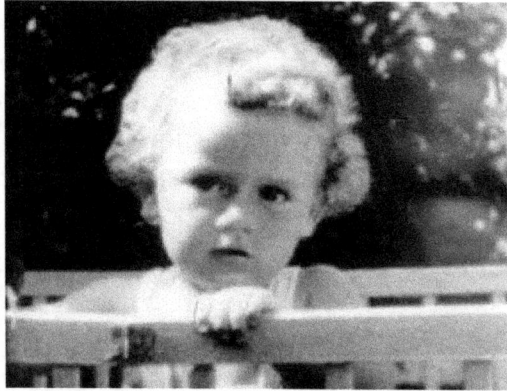

Charles Lindbergh, Jr., 20-month old kidnap victim.

A second note was found on March 6, increasing the ransom amount to $70,000. A third note was received on March 8, saying that a mediator selected by the Lindbergh's was not acceptable. It asked for a note in a newspaper instead.

Dr. John F. Condon, a New York school teacher, published a note in the Bronx Home News that he would be willing to act as a go-between and added $1,000 to the ransom.

A fourth note the following day accepted Dr. Condon's offer.

On May 12, 1932, the body of the child was found, partly buried and badly decomposed. The boy's head was crushed and some body members were missing. He had been dead for at least two months.

A close watch was put out for the ransom money. On May 2, 1933, the Federal Reserve Bank of New York discovered 296 ten-dollar gold certificates, and one $20 gold certificate, all part of the Lindbergh ransom notes.

One of the notes bore the name and address of J.J. Faulkner, 537 West 149th St. The depositor was never located.

A break in the case came when sixteen gold certificates were discovered in the vicinity of Yorkville and Harlem. On September 18, 1934, the assistant manager of the Corn Exchange Bank and Trust Company in New York called the FBI.

He told the agent that a $10 gold certificate was discovered a few minutes previous by a teller. The certificate had been received by a suspicious service station attendant. The attendant recorded the license number of the automobile of the gasoline purchaser.

The number was traced to Bruno Richard Hauptmann, Bronx, New York. He was a native of Saxony, Germany, and had a criminal record. The tool marks on the broken ladder at the kidnap scene matched those of tools owned by Hauptman.

The wood in the ladder matched the wood used in flooring in Hauptmann's attic. Dr. Condon's telephone number and address were found scrawled on a door frame inside a closet. Hauptmann was electrocuted April 3, 1936.

Charles Lindbergh himself was no pillar of virtue it's been disclosed. He had a tangled love life while residing in Germany, where he fathered at least three illegitimate children from three different mistresses.

DNA tests have proved the relationships. Lindbergh apparently had a 17-year relationship with Brigette, the mother of the illegitimate offspring.

Dyrk Hesshaimer, Astrid Bouteuil and David Hesshaimer, the illegitimate children of Charles Lindbergh.

The now-grown children tell that the relationship with their mother endured even after Lindbergh fathered two more illegitimate children with Brigette's sister Marietta.

Lindbergh had previously fathered six children with his wife Anne, with whom he was happily married at the time.

"I am aware that our presence has tainted the image of an impeccable American hero," said Astrid, who was 44-years old at the time she spoke. "But the man once thought of as emotionless and unattainable was in fact a caring and loving father."

2

The Chinese Lady Was A Pirate

Ching Shih: she was the greatest pirate of them all.

Ching Shih was once a prostitute in a small floating brothel in Canton. Yet she succeeded in becoming the most prominent pirate in middle Qing China. She commanded more than 300 junks manned by 20,000 to 40,000 pirates.

Her story is legend. Ching Shih was born in 1775 in Guangdong province. Her name was SHI Xiang Gu. At age 26, she worked in a floating brothel in Canton.

Pirate Xheng Yi found a strong attraction to Ching Shih. There are conflicting stories about how Xheng Yi and Ching Shih were united. Some historians say Xheng Yi sent a raiding party to the brothel to bring Ching Shih to him. Other writers say that Xheng Yi went there himself and proposed marriage to the beautiful young prostitute.

She agreed to his proposal on condition that he gives her an equal share of the plunder and that she be allowed a role in running the organization.

While female pirates were not uncommon off the coast of Asia in the 18th and 19th centuries, it was rare that a brothel prostitute should rise to such a position.

Xheng Yi owned a number of pirate ships known as the Red Flag Fleet. During the next half-dozen years, with the help of the astute management of Ching Shih, Xheng Yi's fleet grew to as many as 600 vessels.

During the next few years, Xheng Yi and Ching Shih made some key alliances. He helped form the Cantonese Pirate Coalition with pirate Wu Shi'er, which brought the number of vessels under their command to 1700-1800 ships.

Chinese pirates awaiting a victim.

Unfortunately, Xheng Yi did not survive when a typhoon struck his ship November 16, 1807.

The artful Ching Shih, rather than stepping aside, convinced Zheng Yi's second in command, 21-year-old Chang Pao to support her in taking over the Red Flag Fleet.

Chang Pao was the son of a fisherman. He was captured at age 15 by Xheng Yi and forced to become a pirate.

He quickly gained favor in the eyes of Xheng Yi for his intelligence, bravery, and skill in a fight. He was adopted as a son by Xheng Yi and Ching Shih.

Soon after Xheng Yi's death, Ching Shih chose Chang Pao to be her second in command. The two became lovers and eventually married.

Chang Pao led the troops in raids while Ching Shih ran the business side of the pirate organization. At the peak of the Red Fleet's success in 1810, Ching Shih and Chang Pao commanded a fleet of 1800 ships.

There were about 17,000 male pirates directly under Ching Shih's control.

Ching Shih didn't just rely on looting, blackmailing and extortion to support her fleet. She set up an ad-hoc government to support her pirates, including establishing laws and taxes.

According to historian Robert Antony, Ching Shih robbed towns, markets, and villages from Macau to Canton.

Because she pretty much controlled the entire criminal element in the South China Sea, Ching Shih could guarantee safe passage through the South China Sea for any merchants willing to pay.

If they didn't pay, they were fair game for Ching Shih's own pirates.

To manage her ruffian pirates, Ching Shih set up a strict system of law within the Red Flag Fleet. These rules spoke for themselves:

"You don't follow the rules or I think you aren't and you get your head chopped off. No exceptions."

She also had a set of specific laws:
- If you disobey an order, you get your head chopped off and body thrown in the ocean.
- If you steal anything from the common plunder before it has been divided up, you get your head chopped off and your body thrown into the ocean.
- If you rape anyone without permission from the leader of your squadron, you get your head chopped off and your body thrown into the ocean.
- If you have consensual sex with anyone while on duty, you get your head chopped off and your body thrown in the ocean and the woman involved would get something heavy strapped to her and tossed in the ocean.
- If you loot a town or ship of anything at all or otherwise harass them when they have paid tribute, you get your head chopped off and your body thrown in the ocean.
- If you take shore leave without permission, you get your head chopped off and body thrown into the ocean.
- Captured ugly women were to be set free unharmed. Captured pretty women could be divvied up or purchased by members of the Red Flag Fleet.

However, if a pirate was awarded or purchased a pretty woman, he was then considered married to her and was expected to treat her accordingly. If he didn't, he gets his head chopped off and body thrown in the ocean.

Ching Shih didn't just restrict herself to sea battles. She used her numerous flat-bottomed boats to good advantage along the rivers and towns along the way.

If an army was raised against her, Ching Shih could cope with the problem. For instance, two towns once banded together, raised an army, and sent it against Ching Shih's forces.

The Red Flag Fleet won the battle and Ching Shih marched her men into both towns and ransacked them, including beheading any males found in the towns.

The Emperor didn't like a pirate, especially a female pirate, controlling such a large portion of his land and subjects. He raised a fleet of ships to attack Ching Shih's fleet. Unbeknownst to the emperor, Ching Shih was a brilliant military strategist.

Rather than running from the Emperor's armada, Ching Shih sailed her ships out to meet it. The Red Flag Fleet easily defeated the Emperor's ships.

Ching Shih was able to steal 63 of the large ships the emperor had sent against her. She also convinced most of the surviving crew members to join her. The crew members were given the choice of joining her or being nailed to the deck by their feet and then beaten to death.

Kwo Lang, the admiral of the fleet sent against Ching Shih, committed suicide before he could be captured by the ruthless Ching Shih.

Without a fleet large enough to send against Ching Shih, the Qing Dynasty enlisted the aid of the super-power British and Portuguese navies. The dynasty also paid large sums to any Dutch vessels willing to help.

These combined forces waged war on Ching Shih for two years without success. She won battle after battle until finally the Emperor decided to take a different tack.

Instead of trying to defeat her, he offered Ching Shih and most of her organization amnesty.

Besides the fate of the loot, one sticking point was the government's demand that the pirates had to kneel before them. For the pirate, to consider kneeling in front of their previously defeated foe was too much to accept.

At first, she rejected the amnesty proposal. Then, in 1810, she unexpectedly showed up at the home of the Governor General of Canton with the intention of working out a peace treaty.

Ching Shih took 17 illiterate women and children and walked into Zhang Bai Ling's office in Canton, unarmed, and began negotiations. She got all she wanted, including the keeping of all of her loot.

The kneeling deadlock was solved by Zhang Bai Ling, acting as a witness at the marriage of Ching Shih and Chang Pao. To receive the government's blessing, the two had to kneel, which was accepted as part of the surrender conditions.

In the agreement, she agreed to disband her fleet, which would, include giving up most of their ships. In return, she and her pirates could keep any loot they had acquired as pirates.

The exceptions were 376 of her crew, of which 126 were executed and the other 250 received some punishment for their crimes.

All the rest were set scot-free. Any who wanted to join the military, including her second in command, her husband Chang Pao.

He was given command of 20 ships in the Qing Dynasty navy to command. Ching Shih was given money to distribute to her crew to offset the cost of them switching from a life at sea to one on the mainland.

Ching Shih negotiated the right to keep the large fortune she had amassed. She also acquired a noble title: "Lady by Imperial Decree". This title gave her various legal protections as a member of the aristocracy.

Ching Shih retired at age 35, opening a gambling house/brothel in Guangzhou, Canton. She managed this operation until her death at age 69.

She also become a mother to at least one son and had become a grandmother.

3

The Crime of
Being a Slave

Slaves in hand bracelets are prepared for loading aboard one of the slave ships.

B ritish Merchants dominated the slave market. The West Indian Atlas of 1796 said 72,000 slaves were carried each year from Africa to the West Indies. Among these, the Danes carry 3,000, the Dutch 7,000, the French 18,000, the Portuguese 8,000, and the English have all the rest.

The British built coastal forts in Africa to hold captured Africans until the slave ships arrived. Merchants obtained the slaves from African chiefs by trading them goods from Europe.

At first, the slaves were mostly soldiers captured in tribal wars. When the demand grew greater, raiding parties were organized to obtain young Africans.

Europeans started taking people from Africa against their will at the end of the Fourteenth Century. They were initially used as servants for the rich.

The Europeans justified the taking of slaves by arguing they were providing the Africans with an opportunity to become Christians. By the end of the 17th Century even the Christian Church endorsed the practice as being a "holy cause".

After the arrival of the Europeans, there was a sharp decline in the local population of most of the islands of the Caribbean Sea. This created a problem for the Europeans as they needed labor to exploit the resources of the islands.

Their solution was to import slaves from Africa. According to Suzanne Schwarz, author of *Slave Captain: The Career of James Irving in the Liverpool Slave Trade*, 37,000 slaving voyages cleared the ports of the Atlantic littoral between the 16th and 19th centuries.

Author Schwartz says that it's estimated that 326,000 slaves were taken from the Bight of Bonny between 1780 and 1800. More than 85 percent of these were carried in British ships.

John Newton was a slave-captain from 1747 to 1754. He said slaves were generally bought and paid for, but if they are lent or trusted on shore, the trader generally leaves a free person, perhaps his own son, as a hostage or pawn for payment.

Olaudah Equiano lived in an Igbo village in the Kingdom of Benin in 1756. He told how he was snatched from his village and enslaved.

"One day, when all our people were gone to their works, only I and my dear sister were left to tend the house. Two men and a woman came over our walls and seized us both.

"Without time to cry out, they *"stopped"* our mouths, and ran off with us to the nearest wood. Here they tied our hands, and continued to carry us as far as they could until night came on when we reached a small house where the robbers halted for refreshment and spent the night.

"We were unbound, but unable to take any food. Our only relief was some sleep. The first object that saluted my eyes was the sea, and a slave ship, which was waiting for cargo."

Hugh Crow worked on several ships as carpenter. He received several offers to go as second mate to the coast of Africa, but had not overcome the prejudice I entertained against the (slave) trade.

He eventually accepted work as a sailor on the slave ship *Elizabeth*. The ship arrived at Annamaboe (English castle). There a strange and weird custom was taking place.

The king of that part of the coast died shortly before the Elizabeth's arrival. This meant all business was suspended. The King had twenty-three wives and custom called for all of them to be put to death when the king died.

Harriet Jacobs, a slave in Edenton, North Carolina, in her book, *"Incidents in the Life of a Slave Girl"*, told of this torture treatment.

The plantation owner had six hundred slaves, many of whom he didn't even know by sight. There was a jail and a whipping post on his grounds. He was wealthy and he could afford to screen both the jail and the whipping post from the public.

One of his favorite punishments, Jacobs said, was to tie a rope around a man's body, suspend him from the ground, and build a fire over which was suspended a piece of fat. As the fat cooked, the scalding drops of fat continually fell on the bare flesh of the slave.

Lewis Clark was a house slave in Kentucky. Ordinary instruments of torture were the raw hide whip, or a bunch of hickory sprouts seasoned in the fire and tied together.

If these were not available, the mistress of the house relished giving a beating with a chair, a broom, tongs, shovel, shears, knife-handle, or an oak club.

Clark said she would often beat slaves with one of these instruments on the hands and on the feet until they were blistered.

Frances Fredric was born a slave in Virginia. She witnessed two slaves, less cowed than the rest, who protested when my master was about to flog them.

"No, massa, we're not going to be flogged so much. We won't submit.

"What is that you say?"

"We are not going to allow you to beat us as you have done."

"How will you prevent it?"

"You'll see, you'll see, massa."

Fredric said he was apparently afraid of them, as when they went home at night, he spoke softly to them. "He told them he only wanted them to do their work, that it would be better if they could get on in the fields without him. Don't hurry yourselves, boys."

For two or three days, the master never went so often among the workers, but when he did, he spoke in a very quiet, subdued manner.

"Mounted Negroes were sent with letters to all the plantations around," Fredric said. "The slaves had been sent to a type of barn where they shell Indian corn.

"Suddenly more than one hundred slaveholders, armed with revolvers, marched from different points, and at one time, evidently agreed upon, surrounded the place where the Negroes were.

All the slaves were ordered out, and the two who had refused to be flogged were made to strip, and my master first had one tied up, and flogged him as hard as he could for some time, the poor slave calling out, "Oh, pray, massa! Oh, pray, massa!"

"My master pausing to take a breath, one of the slaveholders said, "I would not flog him in that way, I would put him on a blacksmith's fire and have the slaves hold him until I blew the bellows to roast him alive."

"Then my master started again and flogged until the poor fellow was one mass of blood and raw flesh. He then tied up the other fellow and flogged him in a similar manner."

The St. Louis Gazette, on November 6, 1845, reported an incident where a wealthy slave owner had a slave boy named Reuben. The boy was almost white. The slave owner branded him on the face with the words, "A slave for life."

Lewis Clark, who worked as a houseboy for a Mrs. Barton, said, "I do not think there were many days, when she was at home, that I, or some other slave, did not receive some kind of beating or abuse at her hands.

"It seemed that she could not live nor sleep unless some poor back was smarting, some head beating with pain, or some eye filled with tears around her."

William Wells Brown was a fugitive slave. He worked for Major Freeland, of Virginia, who was a horse-racer, cock fighter, gambler, and an inveterate drunkard.

Major Freeland had ten or twelve servants in his house. "When he was present, it was cut and slash, knock down and drag out. In his fits of anger, he would take a chair and throw it at a servant. In his more rational moments, when he wished to chastise a servant, he would tie them up in the smokehouse."

After living with Major Freeland for five or six months, Brown ran away. He hid in the nearby woods. One day, he heard the barking and howling of dogs. When they came near, he saw they were bloodhounds used to hunt runaway slaves.

Brown climbed to the top of a tree, but the dogs were there in no time. When the hunters arrived, they ordered Brown to climb down the tree. He did so, knowing it was useless to not follow their orders.

"After I was returned home, I was tied in the smokehouse and severely whipped. The major then sent out his 18-year-old son Robert to see if I was well-cooked."

Harriet Jacobs, writing in "Life of a Slave Girl", told of a slave owner who was vicious in his punishment of his slaves. He kept a pen of hunting dogs that were as vicious as he. When they tracked down a runaway slave, the dogs tore the flesh from the man's bones"

Finally, the slave owner faced his own death, and he didn't do so in a very heroic manner. "His shrieks and groans were so frightful they appalled his friends.

His last words were, "I am going to hell! Bury my money with me."

Moses Roper made several attempts to escape from his cruel master. "Mr. Gooch obtained the assistance of another slave holder, and tied me up in his blacksmith's shop. He gave me fifty lashes with a cow-hide.

"He then put a long chain, weighing twenty-five pounds around my neck and sent me into the field. He followed me with the cow hide, intending to set his slaves to flog me again.

"He then chained me down in a log pen with a forty pound chain and made me sleep on the damp earth all night. In the morning after his breakfast, he came to me, and without giving me any breakfast, tied me to a large heavy barrow, which is usually drawn by a horse.

"He made me drag it to the cotton field for the horse to pull in the field."

W.L. Bost, 88-years-old, was interviewed by the Federal Writers Project in 1937. He was a former slave.

"I remember how they killed one *nigger* whipping him with the bullwhip. Many of the poor niggers were nearly killed with the bullwhip, but this one died.

"He was a stubborn Negro and didn't do as much work as his massa thought he should. He had been lashed a lot before.

"So they take him to the whipping post, and then they strip his clothes off and then the man stand off and cut him with the whip. His back was cut all to pieces. The cuts were about a half-inch apart.

"Then after they whip him they tie him down and put salt on him. Then after he lie in the sun awhile, they whip him again. But when they finish with him, he was dead."

Bost told about the raping of slave women by the slave owners.

"Plenty of the colored women have children by the white men. She knew better than to not do what he say. Didn't have much of that until the men from South Carolina come up here and settle and bring slaves.

"Then they take them very same children what have their own blood and make slaves out of them.

If the missus find out she raise revolution. But she hardly find out.

An armed slave rebellion was the most feared event for a slave holder.

"The white men not going to tell and the nigger women were always afraid to. So they just go on hoping that things won't be that way always.

A slave rebellion is an armed uprising by slaves. Such rebellions have occurred in nearly all societies that practice slavery and are the most feared events for slave-holders.

Little has been said in the history books about slave uprisings in the decades before the American Civil War.

The first slave revolt in North America occurred in 1526. This revolt began in the first Spanish settlement in what is now South Carolina.

Lucas Vasquez de Ayllon, a Spanish colonizer, founded a town near the Pedee River. The settlement consisted of 500 Spaniards and 100 enslaved Africans.

Illness hit the settlement and Ayllon died. The South Carolina Indians became hostile toward the settlement. The enslaved Africans revolted, killing their Spanish masters, and escaped to join the Indians.

In 1687, there was a large-scale plan for rebellion in the Northern Neck region of Virginia. This plan called for the extermination of whites. The plan was discovered and its leaders were arrested an executed.

In 1831, the biggest slave revolt in history was envisioned by Nat Turner and six other slaves. They actually envisioned a crusade that would end slavery in Southampton, Virginia.

The first to be killed in this revolt was Nat Turner's owner Joseph Travis and his entire family. Nat and approximately seventy slaves killed fifty-seven whites—men, women and children.

They left a trail of ransacked plantations, decapitated bodies and heads all across Southampton. Turner declared this was not the intent of the rebellion.

"Indiscriminate slaughter was not their intention. Women and children and men, too, would have been spared if they ceased to resist."

The whites retreated but were also reinforced with local militia. The uprising began on August 21, 1831 and was over by August 23.

Turner's attempts to round up his men were hopeless. Turner was able to elude his pursuers for about thirty days. He was finally caught with only an old sword with which to defend himself.

Nat Turner hid in several different places near the Travis farm, but on October 30 was discovered and captured. His "Confession," dictated to physician Thomas R. Gray, was taken while he was imprisoned in the County Jail.

On November 5, Nat Turner was tried in the Southampton County Court and sentenced to execution. He was hanged, and then skinned, on November 11.

In total, the state executed 55 people, banished many more, and acquitted a few. The state reimbursed the slaveholders for their slaves. But in the hysterical climate that followed the rebellion, close to 200 black people, many of whom had nothing to do with the rebellion, were murdered by white mobs.

In addition, slaves as far away as North Carolina were accused of having a connection with the insurrection, and were subsequently tried and executed.

One revolt reached into high places. In 1858, about 55 slaves on the plantation of the ex-First Lady, Mrs. James K. Polk, near Coffeeville, Mississippi, revolted.

They decided they would no longer endure the whippings and became unmanageable. Overseers assisted by neighbors tried to subdue them, but the slaves armed themselves with axes, hatchets, clubs, scythes and stone.

The revolt ended when 75 armed men came to the plantation from surrounding communities and overpowered the slaves. The leaders of the revolt,

Giles and Emanuel, were tried and convicted and scheduled for execution.

An uncommon occurrence happened in Choctaw County, Mississippi. The slaves on the plantation owned by Nat Best tied up their master and gave him 500 lashes.

Denmark Vesey, a 60-year-old free black carpenter in Charleston, South Carolina, envisioned what would have been the largest slave rebellion.

Vesey could see a massive black uprising throughout the Charleston and surrounding areas. Vesey's conspiracy unraveled when several slaves became informers. Vesey and 130 slaves were arrested as conspirators.

Two-hundred-fifty pike heads such as above were collected for the planned Denmark Vesey uprising. The pike is a pole arm about 16 to 18 feet long with a bladed head.

At the trials, witnesses testified that from 3,000 to 9,000 slaves were in on the plan. The organizers had stashed away 300 daggers and 250 pike heads to wage the uprising.

Of these, 49 were convicted, with 37 executed and 12 pardoned.

We are only a century and a generation away from the age of slavery and Africans are even closer to it as slavery didn't end there until the twentieth century.

As many slaves were made and kept in Africa as were transported as human cargo westward across the Atlantic.

Most African slaves were captured by other Africans and not Europeans. People generally have the image of Europeans landing on the African coast and raiding African villages. This image was re-enforced by the film "Roots", written by African-American Alex Haley.

There were some European raids on African villages, but few slaves were captured this way. This is not to say that the Europeans were not responsible for slavery. The plantations demand for slaves is what drove the slave trade.

The forced removal of up to twenty five million people from the continent of Africa had a major effect on the growth of the population in Africa. It is estimated that in the period from 1500 to 1900, the population of Africa remained stagnant or declined.

Africa was the only continent to be affected in this way. This loss of population and potential population was a factor leading to its economic underdevelopment.

Haiti became the first black republic in the world and first country in the Western Hemisphere to abolish slavery. Haiti is now the poorest country in the Western Hemisphere.

This wasn't always so.

According to Bryan Page, professor and chair of the Department of Anthropology at the University of Miami, Haiti killed off its own wealth.

"In the 17th and 18th centuries, Haiti was by far the richest colony in the entire Americas—including the mineral rich Mexico and Peru. The reason was that Haiti had the greatest agricultural riches. And the other reason was it was essentially a *slave meat grinder*.

French plantation owners in Haiti became extremely wealthy by working their slaves to death. Working conditions were so harsh, said Page that it was inevitable that the slaves would revolt.

"There have never been a people who have thrown off slavery and formed a nation other than Haiti," said Page.

The last recorded slave ship to land on American soil was the *Clotilde*, which, in 1859, illegally smuggled a number of Africans into the town of Mobile, Alabama.

The California Gold Rush brought men from all over the world. Barbary Coast was the section of San Francisco that harbored the red light district. It was rife with gambling, prostitution, pickpockets, and violent crime.

The Barbary Coast was also home to the cribs—low class prostitution houses. In China, girls were not valued. Many girls, even babies, were sold to "entrepreneurs" who took them to America to be used as sex slaves.

In San Francisco, girls were bought and sold. A baby sold for a little over $100. They were then raised to become prostitutes.

VALUABLE GANG OF YOUNG
NEGROES
By JOS. A. BEARD.
Will be sold at Auction,
ON WEDNESDAY, 25TH INST.
At 12 o'clock, at Banks' Arcade,
17 Valuable Young Negroes,
Men and Women, Field Hands.
Sold for no fault; with the best
city guarantees.
Sale Positive
and without reserve!
TERMS CASH.
New Orleans, March 24, 1840.

"These poor creatures are all slaves, bought with a price in China, and imported by degraded men of their own race," according to *Ala California: Sketch of Life in the Golden State*," by Albert S. Evans.

"These girls are held to a long servitude which is a thousand times more hopeless and terrible than the Negro slavery of Louisiana or Cuba could ever be," Evans said.

The author said the girls cost $40 each in Canton, but are valued here at about $400, if passably attractive, young and healthy. "Chinese girls were no more significant, and less valuable, than a horse," said Evans.

4

Notorious Whale
Inspires Moby Dick

A white albino whale whalers named
Migaloo which was harpooned off the
coast of Peru.

Mocha Dick was a notorious sperm whale that lived in the Pacific Ocean off the Island of Mocha, of southern Chile.

Explorer-author Jeremiah N. Reynolds published his account, titled "Mocha Dick: or the White Whale of the Pacific: A Leaf from a Manuscript Journal" in 1839.

Reynolds described Mocha Dick as an "old bull whale of prodigious size and strength...white as wool". Reynolds writes that the whale's head was covered with barnacles, which gave him a rugged appearance.

The author said the whale had a peculiar method of spouting. Instead of projecting his spout obliquely forward, and puffing with a short, convulsive effort, accompanied by a snorting noise as usual with his species, he flung the water from his nose in a lofty, perpendicular, expanded volume.

"Its expulsion produced a continuous roar, like that of vapor struggling from the safety valve of a power engine."

It is believed that Mocha Dick was first encountered prior to the year 1810 off Mocha Island. His survival of the first encounters, coupled with his unusual appearance made him famous among Nantucket whalers.

Many whaler captains tried to hunt him after rounding Cape Horn. He was quite docile, sometimes swimming alongside the ship, but once attacked he retaliated with ferocity and cunning, and was feared by harpooners.

When agitated he would sound then breach so aggressively his entire body would come completely out of the water.

His body was 70 feet long and yielded 100 barrels of oil, along with some ambergris, a substance used in the making of perfumes. Ambergris was sometimes considered more valuable than gold. Mocha Dick had nineteen harpoons in his body.

Mocha Dick was not the only white whale plying the seas. In 1859, a Swedish whaler claimed to have taken a very old white whale off the coast of Brazil. In 1902, whalers harpooned and killed an albino sperm whale near the Azores in the Atlantic Ocean.

A harpoon equipped with an explosive device was used against this gigantic whale which measured 90 feet long. The whale was covered with scars from previous harpoon attacks.

Mocha Dick was one of two whales that inspired Herman Melville's novel Moby Dick. Over the course of the next 28 years, Mocha Dick earned a reputation as one of the most cunning and feared whales in the ocean.

During that time he was spotted and attacked by at least 100 whaling ships. He successfully destroyed 20 of those ships. He escaped all but the last of them.

Author Reynolds said Mocha Dick was killed in 1838 after he appeared to come to the aid of a distraught cow whose calf had just been slain by whalers.

When the cow realized her calf was dead, she turned on the whalers and attempted to destroy their ship. She was unsuccessful, and she in turn was harpooned and mortally wounded.

Mocha Dick decided he would get in on the fray. He destroyed one of the smaller whaling vessels, but was injured by a harpoon in the process. Here is Reynolds's account as gotten from the first mate of the whaling ship:

"Making a leap toward the boat, he darted perpendicularly downward, hurling the after oarsman, who was helmsman at the time, ten feet over the quarter, as he struck the long steering-oar in his descent.

"The unfortunate seaman fell, with his head forward, just upon the flukes of the whale, as he vanished, and was drawn down by suction of the closing waters, as if he had been a feather.

"After being carried to a great depth, as we inferred from the time he remained below the surface, he came up, panting and exhausted, and was dragged on board, amidst the hearty congratulations of his comrades.

"Mocha Dick, overpowered by his wounds, and exhausted by his exertions and the enormous pressure of the water above him, was compelled to turn once more upward for a fresh supply of air.

"And upward he came, shooting twenty feet of his gigantic length above the waves. Hardly had we succeeded in bailing out our swamping boat, when he again darted away, as it seemed to me with renewed energy.]

"For a quarter of a mile he parted the opposing waters as though they had offered no more resistance than air. Our game then abruptly brought to, and he lay as if paralyzed, his massive frame quivering and twitching as if under the influence of galvanism.

"I gave the word to haul on; and seizing a boat spade, as we came near him, drove it twice into him. He wheeled furiously around as though answering our salutation, by making a desperate dash at the boat's quarter.

"We were so near him that to escape the shock of his onset was out of the question. At the critical moment when we expected to be crushed by the collision, his powers seemed to give way.

"The fatal lance had reached the seat of life. His strength failed him in mid-career, and sinking quietly beneath our keel, grazing it as he wallowed along, he rose again a few rods from us, on the side opposite that where he went down."

"Lay around, my boys, and let us set on him! I cried, for I saw his spirit was broken at last.

The other whale that helped inspire Moby Dick was a huge sperm whale that destroyed the Essex in 1820, around 2,000 miles west of South America.

Author Herman Melville learned of the story of the Essex while on a whaling ship. He was only 100 miles from where the Essex was destroyed.

After the Essex was destroyed, the 21 man crew took refuge on three small whaling boats that had almost no supplies to sustain them.

Their choice was to head for known habitable islands that they feared were inhabited by cannibals, 1,200 miles away, or head to South America 2,000 miles away.

The men chose South America. During their journey, they did encounter an island that they stripped of resources to sustain themselves.

They left three men behind there, thinking likely to their doom, to help conserve supplies.

What followed is an incredibly gruesome tale. As they traveled, they steadily lost crew due to lack of nourishment. At a certain point, they were forced to give up burying their men at sea and, instead, began eating them and drinking their blood.

They eventually resorted to not waiting for someone to die, but, rather, drew lots for who was to die and nourish the others with their body.

In the end, 95 days after their ship was destroyed, they were rescued with only five men left alive aboard the two remaining small ships.

Ironically, the three men left on the barren island survived.

5

Magnificent Horses of Myth

The Ghost Stallion

A long time ago, there was a wealthy Indian chief who was despised by his fellow Indians because he was so miserly and cruel. He was called "The Traveler", but no one seems to remember why.

In his younger days, he was a proud warrior who claimed many scalps, many horses and other trophies of value. Many of his possessions came at the expense of the less fortunate. He gambled with younger men who were no match for the Chief's cunning.

The Traveler was admired for his bravery but little loved because of his cruelty and treatment of those of lesser stature. He abused his wives to the point where their parents took them away. His children hated him and he had no love for them.

He cared for one thing. This was his horses. Indeed, they were fine horses as he kept only the best. When a young warrior returned from a raid with a particularly attractive horse, The Traveler couldn't rest until somehow, by hook or crook, he acquired that horse.

At night, when the dance drum was brought out, and the other Indians gathered around it, The Traveler went alone to where his horses were picketed to gloat over his treasures. While shunning all else, he truly loved those horses.

He loved only those that were young, handsome and healthy. Animals that were old, sick or injured received only abuse from The Traveler.

One morning, when he went to the little valley where he kept his horses, he found an ugly, white stallion in his herd of fine mares. The white stallion was old, had crooked legs, a matted coat and was thin and tired looking.

The Traveler flew into a rage. He took his rawhide rope and caught the old horse. With a club, he beat the animal to the ground, even breaking its legs with the club. He left the horse to die.

He returned to his lodge, feeling no remorse whatever for his actions. Later, the greedy chief thought he might be able to use the hide of the animal he had just beaten.

He returned to the place he had left the beast, but to his surprise, the stallion was gone. That night, as The Traveler slept, he had a curious dream.

The white stallion appeared in the dream and turned into a beautiful horse. Shining white, with a long mane and tail, the stallion in the dream was the most beautiful horse The Traveler had ever seen.

The stallion spoke:

"If you had treated me kindly, I would have brought you more horses. But you were cruel to me, so I shall take away the horses you have."

When The Traveler awoke, his horses were gone. All that day, he searched the hills and valleys for his horses, until at last, he fell asleep exhausted.

Again he dreamed. The white stallion asked, "Do you wish to find your horses? They are north, by a lake. You will sleep twice before you come to it."

On awakening the next morning, The Traveler set out northward. After two days, he came to the lake but found no horses.

That night, the Ghost Stallion spoke again in The Traveler's dream.

"Do you wish to find your horses? They are east, in some hills. They will be two sleeps away before you come to them."

On the third day, The Traveler searched the hills and still found no horses.

Night after night, the Ghost Stallion appeared, directing The Traveler to some distant spot. The Traveler grew thin and his feet were sore. Sometimes he would get a horse from some friendly camp, and sometimes he would steal one, to ride in his quest to find his horses.

Always, before morning, the Ghost Stallion and his band would gallop by, The Traveler's horse would break its picket and go with them, leaving him to trod through the hills and valleys on foot.

Never again did he have a horse. Never again did he see his own lodge. He wanders, some old men say, even to this day, searching for his lost horses.

The Enchanted Horse

A very poor old man had a son named Louis. Louis would go hunting to support his parents. One day, while Louis was out hunting, a gentleman came to visit the parents.

The visitor offered the old man a beaver hat full of gold for his son, assuring him that he would take good care of the boy. The boy's duties would be to tend the gentleman's horses.

"In about 20 years, you will get your son back," he promised.

The Enchanted Horse

When the poor man told his wife of the arrangement, she was against it. But goaded by poverty, the old man persuaded her to accept the offer.

The gentleman waited for Louis' return and took him away.

The gentleman showed the boy over his house and gave him permission to eat and drink whatever he wanted.

He also showed him two pots, one full of gold and the other full of silver.

The gentleman warned the boy, "Do not touch either of these."

He then led the boy to the stable and showed him a black horse in the farthest stall, telling him to be very particular in caring for this horse. He was told to wash him three times a day and take him to water three times every day.

The gentleman then pointed to a gray horse. This horse, he told the boy, was to be beaten three times a day, given very little to eat, and given water only once in twenty-four hours. Further, he told the boy to never remove the bridle from the gray horse.

The man then announced that he was going on a journey for a few weeks.

Louis followed the instructions to the letter. Two weeks later, the gentleman returned. He quickly went to the stables to examine his horses. He was pleased with the looks of both the black and the gray horses even though the gray horse looked poorly.

After returning to the house, the gentleman played games with Louis.

Louis noted the man had a knife in his hand. Somehow, Louis' finger was cut by the knife. The gentleman apologized. He took a bottle from his pocket and applied a little liquid to Louis' finger.

The finger healed in minutes, surprising Louis.

The gentleman then informed Louis that he was again leaving on a trip, for a week this time. He instructed Louis to treat the horses the same way he had before.

After the man left, Louis couldn't contain his curiosity. He took the cover off the pots and dipped his finger in the golden liquid. When he pulled it out, lo and behold, his finger changed to gold.

Knowing his master would know he had opened the pots, Louis wrapped his ginger in a piece of rag. He also took pity on the gray horse and did not beat him.

On his return, the man was again pleased with the look of his horses. He noticed that Louis had a rag wrapped around his finger. The master asked what happened. Louis replied that he had cut it.

The gentleman pulled the rag from Louis' finger. Seeing it had turned to gold, he knew what had happened and became very angry. He grasped Louis' finger, twisted it off and threw it into the pot, warning the boy not to touch the pots again.

Again, he played with the boy with his knife out, the man cut Louis' hand again. He pulled the bottle from his pocket and applied a liquid, healing the hand immediately.

He then said he must travel away for a three-week period. He instructed Louis to beat the gray horse five times each day.

That day, as Louis watered the horses, he noticed the gray horse could hardly drink with the bit in its mouth. He took pity on the horse and removed the bridle, allowing the animal to take a good drink.

When the horse lifted his head from the brook, he had a man's face.

He told Louis, "You saved me. If you do as I tell you, we both shall be saved. The master is not a man, but the Devil. He came to my parents as he did yours and bought me with a beaver hat full of money.

"Every time he comes and cuts you, he is trying to see if you are fat enough to be killed. When he returns this time, he will again try you, and, if he finds you are not fat enough, he will turn you into a horse.

"If you are fat enough, he will kill you. If you do as I tell you, Louis, we both shall be saved. Now, feed me as well as you can for two weeks; put my bridle on the black horse, and beat him five times a day. In short, give him the treatment which was destined for me."

Louis followed the gray horse's instructions. The animal began to recover his lost weight and stamina. The black horse, however, lost weight. After two weeks, the gray horse was in good condition and the black horse looked poorly.

"Now," said the gray horse, the Devil suspects that things have not gone properly and he is returning. We must prepare to leave.

"Since his black horse is very swift, you must cut his legs off. Cut the left foreleg off below the knee, and cut the right fore-leg off above the knee. Cut the right hind leg off below the knee, and the left hind leg away above the knee.

"He will then not be able to travel so fast for his legs will be short and of different lengths."

When Louis completed the tasks, the gray horse told him to go to the house and get the pots of silver and gold. When Louis returned, he told the boy to dip his tail in the silver pot, and to dip his mane and ears into the gold one.

"And you dip your hair into the gold pot," the horse told the boy, and stick your little fingers into the metal. Take the saddle and put it on me, but before we start, go into the house and get three grains of black corn which are on his shelf, and take his flint, steel and punk.

"Take also an awl, that round pebble which comes from the seashore, and take that wisp of hay which is pointed."

Louis did as told and then mounted the gray horse and rode away.

Two days later the Devil returned. When he saw the gray horse was gone and the black horse was mutilated, he knew what had taken place. This enraged the Devil so that he began thinking of how he could outwit the fugitive pair. He set out in pursuit.

After several days, the gray horse told Louis, "The Devil and the black horse are pretty close. You did not cut his legs short enough. Give me one of those grains of black corn and I'll go a little faster."

The horse ate the grain and picked up speed. Three days later, he asked for a second grain. The gray horse again increased his speed.

Three days later, the gray horse asked for the last grain. "He is getting very close."

When the gray horse spoke again, he told Louis to throw the awl down behind you. Louis did so. The awl mad a great field of thorn bushes, many miles wide. When the Devil rode up, he was going too fast to stop and rode straight into the thorns.

By the time they extracted themselves from the thorn bushes, Louis and the gray horse again put distance between themselves and the Devil.

Some days later, the gray horse noticed the Devil and the black horse were getting close again.

"Throw back the flint."

When the Devil came up, he faced a high wall of bare rock which extended for miles, allowing Louis and the gray to again put distance between them and the Devil.

Days later, the gray horse again informed Louis, "We have only two things left, and I'm afraid we're going to have a hard time."

Louis said, "We had better throw the punk behind us. He threw it and as it struck the ground, it burst into flame. It started a forest fire that extended many miles.

Still, a few more days and the gray horse said, "I am afraid that he is going to overtake us before we can reach the sea. He is gaining rapidly on us, and is now very close. You had better throw the pebble behind you. It is the only chance we have left."

When the pebble hit the ground, a great lake appeared, extending over many square miles. The Devil was forced to go around it.

As Louis and the gray horse neared the sea, the horse said, "He is still gaining on us and I'm getting very tired."

Looking ahead, Louis could see the ocean. Turning and looking behind, he could see the Devil gaining fast.

Louis did not see at first the advantage of reaching the sea would have, but it soon became apparent. As they gained the seashore, the gray horse instructed, "Throw out the wisp of hay."

Louis did so, and it converted into a bridge. Louis and the gray horse rode out onto the bridge and it folded up behind them. The Devil did not reach the sea until Louis and the gray horse were a safe distance from shore.

"It was very lucky that you took my bridge with you or I would have eaten you two for my dinner," said the Devil.

Louis and the gray horse soon came to a cave. "You stable me in here and go up to the king's house and see if you cannot get work. Warp your head in order that your hair may not be seen. Do the same with your fingers.

A maid noticed Louis as she threw some dishwater out behind the kitchen. She notified the king, who summoned the youth. Louis told the king he wanted work and the king employed him as a gardener.

Every noon, Louis would seclude himself to comb his hair, and then tie his head up into a cloth again.

The princess saw Louis combing his hair one day and was enchanted by his looks. The princess dropped a note to him each day, but they escaped his notice.

Louis decided to visit his horse. Tomorrow, the king will ask you if you are descended from royal blood said the horse. "You tell him you are the child of poor parents. There is a prince who wants to marry the princess, but she does not love him.

"When you go back to work, the princess will drop notes again, but do not touch them. Louis, in time, you will marry her, but do not forget me."

Louis returned to work and again ignored the notes dropped by the princess. The prince came calling again, but the princess would not look at him. The king was distressed and asked why she did not want to see the prince.

She told him she desired to marry the gardener. The king told his wife what the princess had said.

"I think the gardener is a prince in disguise," the king's wife said.

The king called for the gardener, asking him if he were of royal blood. The gardener simply replied, "No, I am the son of poor parents."

The king dismissed him.

The princess, however, contrived a means to marry Louis. She then went back to the king and asked for her dowry.

The king told her that her dowry should be the pig-pen in which he fattened hogs and drove them from the palace with nothing more.

The queen was in tears at the way the king treated their daughter, but he was obdurate.

6

Chief Red Cloud's War

Red Cloud, chief of the Oglala Lakota (Sioux) nation, orchestrated the most successful war against the United States ever fought by an Indian nation.

The war was over the control of the Powder River Country in northeastern Wyoming and southern Montana.

A gold strike in Montana Territory drew a frenzy of gold miners north. A fast and safe route was needed to get miners to the new gold fields.

Mountain Man Jim Bridger warned U.S. officials against establishing a trail though Arapaho and Lakota hunting grounds. Bridger then blazed a trail west of the Bighorn Mountains.

Without regard to Bridger's warning, explorer John Bozeman in 1863 followed the ancient routes through the middle of the Powder River Basin, a move that insured a conflict with the Indians.

Chief Red Cloud

The following year, in 1864, Col. John M. Chivington, headed up a detachment of 700 to 800 Colorado volunteers. He led a reckless and wanton raid on a peaceful Indian camp at Sand Creek near the Arkansas River.

Chivington openly declared, "The Cheyenne will have to be roundly whipped, or completely wiped out, before they will be quiet. I say that if any of them are caught in your vicinity, the only thing to do is kill them."

He was considered one of the most controversial figures in the history of the American West. Chivington soon made good on his genocidal promise.

Mountain man Jim Bridger

During the early morning hours of December 29, 1864, Chivington led a regiment of Colorado volunteers to the Cheyenne's Sand Creek reservation.

There, Chief Black Kettle, a strong advocate of peace between the white men and the Indians, was encamped. Federal army officers promised Black Kettle safety if he would return to the reservation.

Black Kettle was even flying the American flag and a white flag of truce over his lodge. Chivington ordered an attack on the village.

The army lost only nine men, but 200 to 400 Cheyenne and Arapaho men, women and children were massacred. Furious survivors fled north to the Powder River Basin, attacking white settlements and army posts along the way.

Chivington was at first praised for the battle at Sand Creek, and honored with a parade through the streets of Denver.

Soon, however, rumors of drunken soldiers butchering unarmed women and children began to circulate. Chivington was eventually brought up on court-martial charges for his involvement in the massacre.

Colonel John M. Chivington

While Chivington was never punished, he was forced to resign from the Colorado militia, to withdraw from politics, and to stay away from the campaign for statehood.

In the winter of 1865, bands of the Cheyenne, Oglala Lakota and Arapaho tribes set up huge camps on the Tongue and Powder rivers in northern Wyoming.

The following summer, thousands of Indian warriors moved south and attacked Platte Bridge Station, an army post . They killed 26 men. Among those killed was Lt. Caspar W. Collins, for whom Casper, Wyoming is named.

The U.S. military, in 1865, launched the Powder River Expedition. In charge was District of the Plains Commander Brig. General Patrick Conner. His mission was to subdue aggressive Indian forces in the Powder River country.

Connor's 2,600 men were organized into three widely separated units, traversing hundreds of miles of what would later become Montana and Wyoming.

The army troops were disorganized and suffered from terrible weather. They were harassed by Indians who avoided pitched battles. One group, led by Conner, followed the Bozeman Trail. They built Fort Conner on the Powder River east of present-day Kaycee, Wyoming.

When the expedition began, Conner's orders to his officers were, "You will not receive overtures of peace or submission from Indians, but will attack and kill every male Indian over twelve years of age." His superiors countermanded this order.

Most of the time, Connor's three units were on the defensive. They were forced to fend off Indian raids on their horses and supply wagons which left many soldiers on foot, in rags, and reduced to eating raw horse meat.

The expedition was a dismal failure for Connor and his troops, many of whom were anxious to get home now that the Civil War was over.

In 1851, the U.S. Interior Department summoned various Indians to Fort Laramie to sign a treaty. Chief Conquering Bear with Oglala and Brule Sioux gathered near Fort Laramie in 1854 to receive the promised allotments of food from the government.

The supplies were delayed.

At the same time, a sickly, half-starved cow, belonging to the Hans Peter Olson Company of Mormons who were passing through the area, wandered into the Indian camp.

The Indians regarded the cow as abandoned and used it to provide sustenance.

The Mormons complained to the Military and demanded the return of the cow. Young West Point graduate Brevet Second Lt. John L. Grattan took a company of soldiers to the camp of Chief Conquering Bear and demanded that the Indian who took the cow be turned over to the military. Chief Conquering Bear refused, but offered instead compensation in the form of a horse, which was deemed more valuable than the cow.

Grattan refused the offer.

As Chief Conquering Bear turned to walk away, one of Grattan's soldiers shot the Indian. In the ensuing fire fight, Grattan and all but one of his men were killed. The one who survived that battle had his tongue cut out and subsequently died in the Fort Laramie hospital

Among those present was a young Indian boy who would later be known as Red Cloud.

He was born Mahpiya Luta in 1822 near North Platte, Nebraska. His mother was Walks As She Thinks, an Oglala Lakota, and his father was Lone Man, a Brule Lakota chief.

In the tradition of the matrilineal Lakota, the children belong to the mother's clan and people. Red Cloud was mentored by his maternal uncle, Old Chief Smoke.

When his parents died, Red Cloud was brought into the Smoke household. At a young age, Red Cloud fought against neighboring Pawnee and Crow, gaining considerable war experience.

Government officials determined that the Indians needed to be punished for the massacre of Grattan and his company. Col. William S. Harney, who previously served in the Seminole Wars in Florida, set out on an expedition to inflict punishment.

Harney's forces included 600 men, consisting of the 2nd Dragoons, five companies from the 6th Infantry, one company from the 10th Infantry and a battery of the 4th Artillery.

The armed militants came upon the camp of Chief Little Thunder at Blue Water Creek, near Ash Hollow, Nebraska. When the Indians began to flee, Harney deceived Little Thunder with a white flag of truce.

Harney's troops then surrounded the camp and killed the men, women and children within. A young topographic engineer named G.K. Warren reported, "The sight was heart-rending—wounded women and children were crying and moaning, horribly mangled by the bullets."

At the same time, the U.S. War Department sent Colonel Henry B. Carrington into the Powder River Basin with 700 troops. This angered Oglala Chief Red Cloud and he refused to sign the treaty.

Thus began what became known as "Red Cloud's War".

Red Cloud's War was the name the U.S. Army gave to a series of conflicts fought with American Indian Plains tribes in the Wyoming and Montana territories. The battles were waged between the Northern Cheyenne, allied with Lakota and Arapaho bands.

Carrington moved Fort Connor downriver and renamed it Fort Reno. He then built Fort Phil Kearny on the Piney Creek near present-day Story, Wyoming. This was followed by the building of Fort C.F. Smith in southern Montana Territory.

In December, a band of Oglala and Minniconjou Lakota warriors led by Red Cloud, Crazy Horse and High-Back-Bone lured Captain W.J. Fetterman over a rise near Fort Phil Kearny. It was a trap.

Within half an hour, Fetterman and all 80 of his men were dead. Their bodies were stripped, scalped and mutilated by the Indians.

Red Cloud, Crazy Horse and High-Back-Bone led another attack near Fort Phil Kearny. They ambushed a woodcutting party and its military escort about five miles from the fort.

The outcome here was different than the Fetterman massacre.

Thirty-two army men lifted the wagon boxes from 14 wagons. They arranged them into a make-shift corral.

Thus fortified, the soldiers fired their new Springfield-Allen breech-loading rifles faster than the Indians could reload their own guns. Four members of the wood-cutting party were killed. Estimates of Indian deaths ranged from 60 to 1500.

After these battles and several smaller attacks, another treaty meeting was set at Fort Laramie. The 1868 treaty granted the land north of the Platte River from the Bighorns to South Dakota Territory to the Indians.

Cheyenne and Arapaho chiefs meeting at the Camp Weld Council on September 28, 1864.

Troops pulled out of Fort Kearny. As the soldiers marched away, smoke billowed up behind them as Cheyenne warriors burned the fort to the ground.

This marked the end of Red Cloud's war.

7

The Strange Life
Of Howard Hughes

Howard Hughes

Howard Hughes became a millionaire at age 18. Both his mother and his father died the previous year and Hughes was awarded 75 percent of their estate.

He disdained the idea of running his father's Hughes Tool Company, choosing instead to go to Hollywood where he would produce movies.

Howard Hughes was involved in a near-fatal aircraft accident on July 7, 1946. Hughes was performing the first flight of the prototype U.S. Army Air Force reconnaissance aircraft, the XF-11.

An oil leak resulted in one of the contra-rotating propellers reversing pitch, causing the craft to yaw sharply and lose altitude. He tried to save the aircraft by landing it at the Los Angeles Country Club golf course.

He came up short of the golf course and landed in the middle of the Beverly Hills neighborhood surrounding the golf course.

Hughes managed to pull himself out of the flaming wreckage. He lay beside the burning craft until Lt. Col. Charles E. Meyer, who was in the area, rescued him.

His injuries were serious. He had a crushed collar bone, multiple cracked ribs, a crushed chest with a collapsed left lung, which shifted his heart to the right side of the chest cavity.

As Hughes lay in his hospital bed, he did not like the bed's design. He called in plant engineers to design a "tailor-made" bed, equipped with hot and cold running water. The bed was built in six sections and operated by 30 electric motors with push-button attachments.

The bed was designed by Hughes to alleviate the pain cause by moving with his severe burn injuries. Despite the fact he was never able to use the bed, it served as the prototype for the modern hospital bed in use by modern hospitals today.

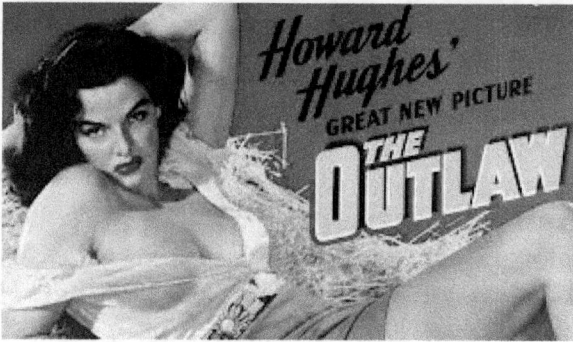

Jane Russell in "The Outlaw".

Howard Hughes was born December 24, 1905, at Humble, Texas. He was one of the wealthiest people in the world when he died April 5, 1976 at age 70. His wealth was estimated at $1.5 billion.

His father, Howard R. Hughes, Sr. was a brilliant engineer. He patented the two-cone roller bit which allowed rotary drilling for petroleum. He made the shrewd decision to commercialize the invention by leasing the bits instead of selling them. He founded the Hughes Tool Company in 1909.

Howard's father died leaving seventy five percent of his fortune to his son, who was then only 19 years old.

Howard married Ella Botts Rice, of Houston, soon after his father's death. They moved to Los Angeles where Howard hoped to make a name for himself producing movies.

Whether it was Hughes philandering ways or simply her dislike for the Hollywood scene, his wife returned to Houston and filed for divorce.

Hughes' first two films were financially successful. He made a name for himself when he produced "The Outlaw" with Jane Russell, whose costumes aroused the ire of censors.

Hughes designed a special bra for Russell to wear in the film. She never wore it because of its improper fit. In his book, "Howard, the Amazing Mr. Hughes", Noah Dietrich wrote that Hughes genuinely liked Jane Russell, but never sought a romantic involvement with her.

Russell's own autobiography, however, claims that Hughes did try to bed her after a party, but Russell, who was married at the time, refused him. Hughes promised it would never happen again.

In 1936, when Hughes was 31, he struck and killed a pedestrian in Los Angeles. Although Hughes was certified sober at the hospital where he was taken, an attending doctor made a note that Hughes had been drinking.

A witness to the accident claimed Hughes was driving erratically and too fast, and that the victim was standing in the safety zone of a streetcar stop.

By the time of the coroner's inquiry, the witness had changed his story and claimed the victim had moved directly in front of Hughes' vehicle. Hughes was held blameless by the coroner's jury.

As early as the 1930s, Hughes displayed signs of mental illness, primarily obsessive-compulsive disorder. Friends noted that he became obsessed with the size of peas, one of his favorite foods. He used a special fork to sort them by size.

While directing the film, *The Outlaw*, Hughes became fixated on a minor flaw in one of Jane Russell's blouses. He claimed the fabric bunched up along a scene and gave the appearance of two nipples on each breast.

He became so upset by the matter that he wrote a detailed memorandum to the crew on how to fix the problem.

In 1947, after his near-fatal plane crash a year earlier, Hughes told his aides he wanted to screen some movies at a film studio near his home.

He stayed in the studio's darkened screening room for more than four months, never leaving. He subsisted entirely on chocolate bars, chicken and milk. He relieved himself in the empty bottles and containers.

Hughes was surrounded by dozens of Kleenex boxes, which he continuously stacked and rearranged. He wrote detailed memos to his aides on yellow legal pads giving them explicit instruction not to look at him, to respond when spoken to, but otherwise not to speak to him.

Throughout this period, he sat fixated in his chair, often naked, continuously watching movies.

When he finally emerged in the spring of 1948, his hygiene was terrible. He had not bathed nor cut his hair and nails for weeks. This may have been due to allodynia—pain upon being touched.

After leaving the screening room, Hughes moved into a bungalow at the Beverly Hills Hotel. He also rented out several other rooms for his aides, his wife, and his numerous girlfriends.

His erratic behavior continued as he would sometime sit naked in his bedroom with a pink hotel napkin placed over his genitals, watching movies. Some believe he did this because clothing could trigger the allodynia.

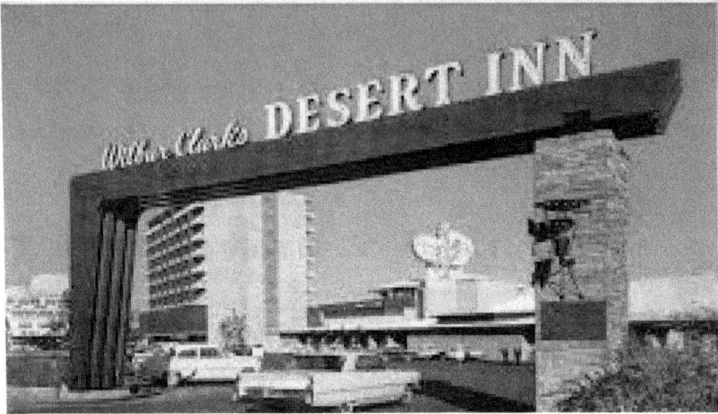

The Desert Inn

It is estimated that in one year, he spent $11 million at the hotel.

He became obsessed with his home state. At one time, he began purchasing all restaurant and four star hotels within the borders of Texas. Ownership of the restaurants was placed in the hands of the Howard Hughes Medical Institute and all licenses were resold shortly afterward.

Hughes insisted on using tissues to pick up objects. This was an effort to insulate himself from germs. If he noticed dust, stains or other imperfections on people's clothes, he demanded that they take care of them.

He became addicted to codeine, which he injected to relieve the pain that was the result of his numerous aircraft crashes. He injected the codeine intramuscularly.

His chronic pain was so severe that even the act of tooth brushing was painful, so he avoided it. Hughes had his hair and nails trimmed once a year.

As he grew older, he began moving from one hotel to another, taking up residence in the top floor penthouse. His entourage of personal aides always moved with him.

When Hughes first came to Las Vegas in 1966, he leased the top floor of the Desert Inn. A short time later, the casino owners tried to evict him so he bought the hotel for $13.6 million and threw the casino managers out in the street.

Hughes later purchased the Castaways, Sands, Silver Slipper, Frontier Hotel, and Landmark hotels.

In 1966, he arrived in Las Vegas by rail car and moved into the *Desert Inn*. He refused to leave the hotel, and to avoid conflicts with the owners, he bought the hotel.

The hotel's eighth floor became the nerve center for his empire. He bought several other hotels between 1966 and 1968, including the Castaways, New Frontier, the Landmark Hotel and Casino, and the Sands. He bought the small Silver Slipper casino so he could reposition its neon silver slipper sign. It had been keeping him awake at night.

Hughes vast holdings were overseen by "The Mormon Mafia", so-called because so many Latter-Day Saints were on the committee. In addition to supervising day-to-day business operations and Hughes' health, they went to great pains to satisfy his every whim.

He became fond of Baskin-Robbins' Banana Ripple ice cream. His aides sought to buy a bulk shipment for him. They learned that Baskin-Robbins had discontinued the flavor.

They put in a request for the smallest amount the company could provide for a special order of 200 gallons and had it shipped from Los Angeles. A few days after the shipment arrived, Hughes announced he was tired of the flavor and only wanted Chocolate Marshmallow ice cream.

The Desert Inn distributed free servings of Banana Ripple ice cream to casino customers for a year.

Howard Hughes spent most of his later years lying naked in bed in darkened hotel rooms that he considered were germ-free zones.

He wore tissue boxes on his feet to protect them from any germs that might be on the carpet. If someone near him became ill, he burned his clothing.

After Hughes' death, estate attorney, Raymond D. Fowler, PhD, was asked to conduct a psychological autopsy to determine Hughes' mental and emotional condition in his last years.

Fowler's findings were used in civil lawsuits filed by people who made claims to the billionaire's estate. Hughes had died without a will. Fowler worked full time for one year conducting the autopsy and then on and off for five years following.

He interviewed Hughes' staff, evaluated newspaper accounts, court dispositions, old letters Hughes' mother wrote about him and other documents. Fowler looked at transcripts from Hughes' phone calls and at his pilot logs.

Fowler said, "A picture gradually emerged of a young child who pretty much was isolated and had no friends, and a man increasingly concerned with his own health."

Fowler's research led him to believe that Hughes's fear for his health most likely emerged from his childhood. "His mother was constantly worried about his exposure to germs."

She was concerned that he might contact polio, a major health threat at the time. She checked him every day for diseases and was cautious about what he ate.

In adolescence, Hughes was paralyzed for several months and unable to walk. After a few months, the symptoms disappeared. Dr. Fowler believes the condition, for which no physical basis was found, was psychologically based.

Hughes' concern about germs continued throughout his life. For example, he wrote a staff manual on how to open a can of peaches. The manual included directions on removing the label, scrubbing the can down until it was bare metal, washing it again and pouring the contents into a bowl without touching the can to the bowl.

Ironically, in his later years, he neglected his own personal hygiene, rarely bathing or brushing his teeth. Yet, he ordered his staff to wash their hands several times and to layer their hands with paper towels when serving his food.

"He didn't believe germs could come from him," said Fowler. "He was convinced that he was going to be contaminated from the outside."

Howard Hughes was a millionaire at age 18 (some accounts say 19).

Both his mother and his father died leaving 75 percent of the family fortune. (The other 25 percent went to relatives)

Hughes arrived in Las Vegas in the dark of night on a private holiday. At the time, he harbored no intentions of buying a hotel, according to Robert A. Maheu, Hughes' longtime confidante.

In the early 1950s, he acquired some 40 square miles near Las Vegas from the Bureau of Land Management. He traded 73,000 acres of desert land in five Northern Nevada counties for the federal parcel.

Hughes Nevada holdings reached $300 million in value before his buying spree stopped.

In 1966, Hughes came to Las Vegas on a two-car private train. His aides whisked him to the Desert Inn. When Moe Dalitz, then the manager if the Desert Inn asked Hughes to vacate the penthouse because some high-paying guests were arriving for the New Year's Eve party, Hughes responded by buying the hotel for $13 million.

He soon after added the Sands, for $14.6 million, the Frontier, for $23 million, and the unfinished Landmark, which had stood empty for eight years. He paid $17 million for the Landmark.

Despite Hughes' refusal to be photographed, fingerprinted or to fill out financial disclosure papers, he got a license to operate the Desert Inn from the Nevada Gaming Commission.

His father, who invented popular rotary drill bit, developed Hughes Tool Company which was worth millions. Rather than run his father's business, young Howard fled to Hollywood to pursue his two passions, movies and aviation.

He produced a few films, some successful and other losing money. He decided he wanted to make an epic World War 1 flying film. It was called *"Hell's Angels"* and made a star of Jean Harlow.

The film cost so much to produce, about $4 million, it was one of the most expensive films af that time. While it may not have been a financial success, it did make Howard Hughes a major player on the Hollywood scene.

His marriage was failing, so Hughes took advantage of the stunning string of actresses waiting in the wings. He dated such beauties as Bette Davis, Katherine Hepburn, Ginger Rogers, Gene Tierney, Ava Gardner and his leading lady Jean Harlow.

Gene Tierney, with whom Howard remained good friends even after his failed attempts to seduce her, said, "I don't think Howard could love anything that did not have a motor in it."

Tierney's daughter, Daria, was born deaf and blind and with severe learning disabilities. The illness was due to Tierney being exposed to rubella during her pregnancy.

Howard Hughes saw to it that Daria received the best medical care with all expenses paid.

In 1936, Hughes' automobile struck and killed Gabriel S. Meyer at the corner of 3rd Street and Lorraine in Los Angeles. A witness claimed Hughes was driving erratically and too fast. An attending physician at the hospital where Hughes was taken made a note that Hughes had been drinking.

Hughes was booked on suspicion of negligent homicide and held overnight in jail until his attorney, Neil McCarthy, obtained a writ of habeau corpus for his release pending an inquest.

The witness to the accident changed his story at the coroner's inquiry, saying the victim had moved directly in front of Hughes' car.

Hughes was held blameless for Meyer's death.

In 1957, Hughes married actress Jean Peters. They met in the 1940s before Peters became a film actress. She at first rejected his proposal, saying it could not combine with her career.

In 1970, Peters filed for divorce. She requested a lifetime alimony of $70,000 per year, adjusted for inflation, and waived all claims to Hughes' estate.

Hughes offered her a settlement of more than a million dollars, which she declined. Hughes did not asked for a confidentiality agreement as a condition of the divorce.

Aides say he never ever spoke ill of her. She refused to discuss her life with Hughes and declined several lucrative offers from publishers and biographers.

Peters would state only that she not seen Hughes for several years before their divorce and had only dealt with him by phone.

Melvin Dummar's story that he picked up a disheveled Howard Hughes lying at the side of Highway 95 in Nevada was shot down by a Nevada jury.

The jury ruled that the handwritten will entitling Dummar to one-sixteenth of the Hughes estate was a forgery.

A veteran Las Vegas detective has now found new evidence that Dummar was telling the truth about finding Howard Hughes along a highway.

Gas station operator Melvin
Dummar claims he saved Howard
Hughes' life when the billionaire
was lying on a stretch of Nevada
highway.

Dummar claims that while driving in rural
Nevada one night in December of 1968, he pulled
off the road to urinate. He says he found a scraggly
bearded man lying injured along the desert road.

The man asked Dummar to drive him to the
Desert Inn in Las Vegas. "I thought he was a bum.
I lent him some money."

Dummar claimed a handwritten will by Howard
Hughes was brought to him at the gas station
where he worked by a mysterious stranger. He says
he dropped the will off at a LDS (Latter Day
Saints) Church headquarters.

He says he didn't know if the will was the real thing or a hoax. Not knowing what to do with it, he delivered to the church headquarters.

After a trial that last three months, a jury said the will was a forgery. Dummar said, "I wouldn't have had a chance even if God himself delivered the will. So many people thought I was a con artist or a scammer, and they treated me like a criminal."

Now, retired FBI agent Gary Magnesen thinks he has proof that Dummar was telling the truth. After he retired, someone asked him to look into Dummar's story.

"I thought Melvin was a kook. It didn't make any sense at all. Why was Howard Hughes out in the desert in the middle of nowhere? Why did he look like that? It didn't make any sense at all," said Magnesen.

Magnesen spent two years investigating the case. He said he discovered three important new witnesses who prove beyond a reasonable doubt that Dummar's story is true.

The three witnesses include employees of the reclusive billionaire, who said Hughes told them he was picked up by Melvin after the incident occurred.

One witness is pilot Roberto Deiro, who says he secretly flew Howard Hughes to various places. One such flight was to the Cottontail Ranch, a whorehouse. He said he wanted to visit his favorite prostitute, a girl called "Sunny".

While waiting for Hughes, Deiro had several drinks and passed out. When he awoke at 5 a.m., he asked where Hughes was and they told him he had gone.

Magnesen found a 1968 deed that may help explain the desert encounter between Hughes and Dummar. The deed shows that the Hughes organization purchased an interest in 32 mines located on the very dirt road where Dummar says he found the stranded Hughes.

Another Hughes employee, one LaVane Forsythe, says that in 1972, Hughes handed him the document now identified as the "Mormon Will". He was told to deliver it to Dummar after Hughes' death.

When the furor over the will subsided it left the Dummar's broke and the newly constructed Highway 95 bypassed Dummar's service station.

Magnesen has written a book "The Investigation: A Former FBI Agent Uncovers the Truth Behind Howard Hughes, Melvin Dummar, and the Most Contested Will in American History".

While making the film *"Hell's Angels"*, Hughes figured if he was going to have the respect of aviators he would have to be a flyer himself.

He went to Clover Field in Santa Monica to take flying lessons. He was assigned 21-year-old instructor Chuck La Jotte. Hughes immediately said that this wasn't going to work. "He can't train me. He's too young!"

The flying school then assigned him the veteran pilot Moye Stephens. Each morning the two spent several hours flying. The inquisitive Hughes would yell out technical questions above the noise of the airplane engine.

Because Hughes had a high degree of deafness, the constant yelling or questions often irritated Moye Stevens.

Jean Harlow

While taking his flying lessons, Hughes met Frank Tomick, the fearless pilot and aerial stunt coordinator for the movie *"Wings"*.

Hughes wanted a British setting for his *"Hell's Angels"* movie. He put Tomick in charge of obtaining, on an open budget, every British and German aircraft he could find.

In those days, it was difficult to find foreign aircraft in the U.S. In many cases when such aircraft was needed, planes were repainted or remodeled to provide simulated versions. Curtiss Jennies were designed to look like British Avros; a Sikorsky had to be faked to resemble a German Gotha bomber.

Hughes eventually acquired about 45 airplanes. He bought a cow pasture next to Van Nuys and named it Caddo Field. He hired a ground crew and built hangars in administration buildings.

He grabbed onto property at Inglewood Field, Now Los Angeles Airport, and built an imitation headquarters of the British Royal Flying Corps. For a German aircraft base, he acquired considerable acreage near Chatsworth, California, north of San Fernando Valley.

Hughes hired German Zeppelin experts to come to Hollywood and build sets which would be exact replicas of the airships' interiors. The film maker turned aviator worked nonstop drafting storyboards on huge sheets of architect paper for aerial combat scenes.

According to author Charles Higham, in his book, *"Howard Hughes, the Secret Life"*, Hughes and start actor Ben Lyon, became close friends.

Lyon was a man after his own heart. He whisked Hughes off to parties where they picked up women, took them to Lyon's home and made love to them as a foursome."

Higham said Hughes was known to be a bisexual and he had a close relationship with gay actor John Darrow, who would play a German in Hughes' movie.

Since the pilots Hughes dealt with were heterosexual, according to biographer Lawrence Quirk, he would compel very young and inexperienced mechanics or their aides to give him satisfaction. It is believed he paid them, either in cash or advancement.

Before his *Hell's Angels* could be released, Hughes knew it would fail unless sound was added. He hired British theater director James Whale to come to Hollywood to ensure authenticity of the scenes set in London.

Hughes fired Greta Nissen from the starring role in Hell's Angels because her accent was too Norwegian for a British aristocrat. He replaced her with Jean Harlow.

Howard Hughes was corrupt in both his personal and his business associations. He was a well-known bisexual and had relationships with a string of well-known male movie stars. These included Cary Grant, Randolph Scott, and Tyrone Power.

He bedded equally famous actresses, including Katherine Hepburn, Bette Davis, Gene Tierney, Ginger Rogers, Linda Darnell and Ida Lupino, to mention only a very few that succumbed to the charms or the wealth of Howard Hughes.

Some male Hollywood stars rejected his advances. Robert Taylor turned him down, as did Errol Flynn, who referred to Hughes as a "deaf haddock".

Several of Hughes' Hollywood lovers faulted the magnate's love-making ability, both in potency and in artistry. His desire was only to satisfy himself.

Higham wrote, "It would certainly fit with Hughes' personality that he was the dominant partner, anonymously male and powerful, submitting men to ropes, handcuffs, gags, and chains; in that murky world, in the near-darkness, it was not necessary to be a great cocksman; relief was often obtained by mutual or individual masturbation."

J. Edgar Hoover was bugging Hughes' telephones. He was on Hoover's watch list for buying Elliott Roosevelt's attention in an aircraft deal with the government. He also got Hoover's attention with his attempts to win favor with senators, congressmen, Air Force and Army bigwigs.

Through all of those sexually related years, according to author Higham, Hughes kept buying Air Corps, Army, and presidential contacts who could help him sell planes to the government.

Famed columnist Westbrook Pegler wrote about parties for nine sponsored by Hughes at the Stork Club; about a $132 pair of nylon stockings for Faye Emerson, the actress who married Elliot Roosevelt after dallying with Hughes for a period.

Roosevelt stayed at the Beverly Hills Hotel at Hughes' expense for weeks. He merely signed his bill: "Mail to Hughes Aircraft." A senate investigative committee found that Hughes had paid Elliot Roosevelt $75,000 for his support with government buyers.

Substantial evidence exists showing Howard Hughes may have contracted the AIDs virus prior to his death.

It is known that Hughes suffered from symptoms common to AIDs sufferers: dehydration, weight loss and fevers.

If he did indeed have AIDs it is believed he got it through the numerous blood transfusions he received during the 1960s and 1970s, according the Charles Higham, author of "Howard Hughes, The Secret Life".

One secret, of which only his closest friends was aware, is that Hughes was afflicted with deafness at an early age. It plagued him throughout his life.

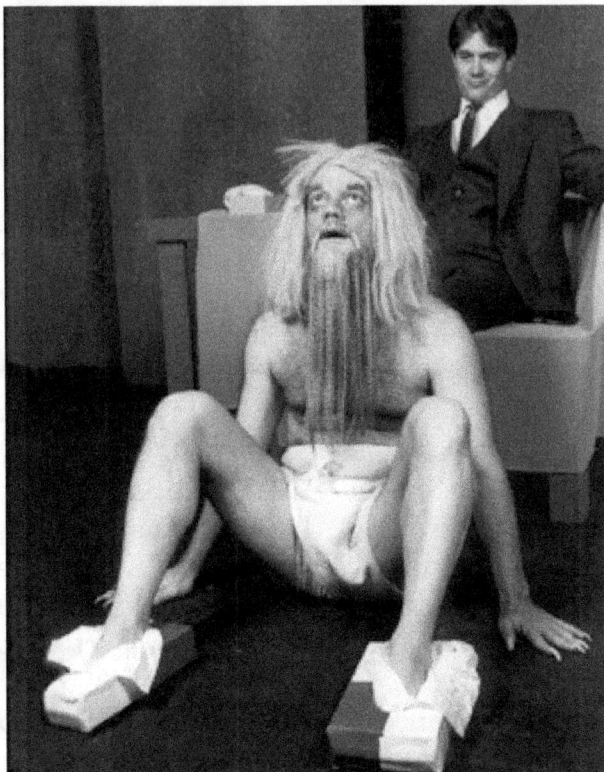

Howard Hughes wore empty Kleenix boxes on his feet so he wouldn't come in contact with the carpet.

He heard a continual ringing in his ears. He was too proud to wear a hearing aid. Consequently, the only time he was truly happy was in the cockpit of a plane. There, the ringing in his ears seemed to cease.

After he was forced to relinquish his control of TWA, Hughes became increasingly paranoid and his behavior turned more and more eccentric. He began alienating his closest advisors and executives.

Although Hughes had clearance to view top-secret government information because of the multimillion dollar defense contracts with Hughes Tool Company, he didn't agree with government policies.

He especially took issue with the government's nuclear explosions at the Nevada Test Site, sixty five miles northwest of Las Vegas. While living at the Desert Inn, he tried but failed to get the explosions halted.

Another of his idiosyncrasies involved Robert Maheu one of his chief advisors. Despite the services that Maheu provided for Hughes, the two never ever met face-to-face.

Hughes only communicated with him by telephone or through memos. His reticence to meet with Maheu apparently involved Hughes' excessive paranoia about germs.

Hughes even wrote directives to his staff about how many tissues they needed to use to carry items in and out of his suite.

After four years in Las Vegas, Hughes left abruptly. On Thanksgiving Eve, 1970, he was carried out of the Desert Inn on a stretcher, driven to Nellis Air Force Base in an unmarked van, and flown by private jet to Resorts International's Britannia Beach hotel in the Bahamas.

Robert Maheu was fired by Hughes when he left Las Vegas. Maheu told the Las Vegas Sun in 2004, "I often said after I got off the phone with him that I just finished talking to the poorest man in the world. He was so unhappy."

8

A Harrowing Gold Prospector's Tale

Thomas Bay in Alaska.

Thomas Bay is sometimes referred to as the Bay of Death or Devil's Country.

The bay lies northeast of Petersburg, Alaska and is named for U.S. Navy officer Charles M. Thomas.

Thomas Bay is known for its rich gold and quartz deposits, and for being inhabited with "devil creatures".

In 1750, a tiny native village on Thomas Bay was completely buried by a large landslide. It killed 500 villagers. Since that time, the land has thought to have been cursed.

The story was originally written by Harry Colp, one of four gold prospectors that were batching together in a shack at Wrangle Alaska. Harry listed his companions only John, Charlie and Fred.

"Charlie came into the shack one night all excited. He said, "Fellows, I have been on the trail of an old Indian for the last month trying to get him to tell me where he picked up a piece of free gold quartz he has at his camp.

"I've never said anything about it before," Charlie continued, "because I wanted to get the story from him first. Today he spilled the beans."

The Indian told Charlie to go up to Thomas Bay and camp on Patterson River on the right side, travel upriver for about eight miles and then turn to the high mountains after traveling about a mile and a half.

He said I would find a lake shaped like a half-moon. The Indian said, "Plenty of stone like I found on a slide there."

Harry Colp said, "Well, it's well-known that a prospector is ready to stampede on a whisper of gold any place and we were no exceptions. We talked the matter over"

We decided that while Charlie was gone to Thomas Bay, John Fred and myself would hustle work somewhere for another grub stake and to pay the old one off.

In the fore part of May, Charlie loaded his outfit into a canoe and having favorable weather, left Wrangle for Thomas Bay.

Charlie had three months supplies but he was to come back sooner if he found anything. If he didn't show up, we would put a search out for him.

John and Fred got a job cutting wood and I got in the Wrangle sawmill, Harry wrote. Things were fine until the first part of June, when on a Sunday in the later afternoon, in walks Charlie without a coat or hat and looking as if he had been through hell.

He didn't give us a greeting whatever. He just heaved a piece of quartz over into a corner of the room and said, "Get me something to eat. I'm all in and want to rest."

After he had eaten, he turned in without telling us a thing about the trip.

We picked up the piece of quartz, Harry wrote, and "Say, boy, it sure was a pretty thing to look at for a prospector. It was shot through with gold specks just like a badly freckled faced kid. Were we excited? I'll say we were!

"Just before dark we walked down to the beach to bring up Charlie's outfit as he came up to the shack with only that piece of quartz in his hand. But there wasn't a thing in his canoe except the oars."

A kayak route to Thomas Bay

We three didn't get much sleep that night, but Charlie never stopped sawing wood. We even had hard work getting Charlie up for breakfast the next morning.

When he did roll out, he just ate, borrowed a coat and hat and left the house without saying a word or even answering one question out of the many we put to him."

The three of us, Harry said, were excited, feeling we were worth a fortune, and did not go to work that day. We just sat around the shack and passed that blamed piece of rock back and forth while we talked and waited for Charlie.

Along in the afternoon, Charlie came in and said, "Fellows, the SS Drigo will be in on her way south early tomorrow morning. Can you give me enough money for my ticket to Seattle? I'm through with Alaska and never want to see it again."

He said, "I'll tell you about my trip to Thomas Bay and where I found the quartz, but my advice to you is to forget about it. It will never do you any good and will only cause you a lot of mental and physical pain.

"I would never open my lips about this trip or what I found, but if you promise never to mention my name in connection with what I tell you or mention the name of Thomas Bay to me again, I'll give you the straight of my experience up there."

Charlie said, "Judge for yourselves as to my saneness, because this is the most astounding thing you ever heard and as far as I am concerned, is beyond me to reason it out."

Charlie told this story:

The first night after leaving Wrangle found me in Ideal Cove. Next night I reached Muddy River in time to make camp again. The third night I hit Ruth Island in Thomas Bay.

I spent the day looking up Patterson River for a suitable place for a good camp, which I found a quarter mile up from tidewater on the right hand side, looking up the river.

I broke camp on Ruth Island the next day and moved up to the place I picked out the day before. I put up my tent, packed up my outfit and left the canoe on the river bank.

The next day I spent cooking beans, cutting wood and making things comfortable for a long stay. As it looked like rain, I wanted to get thing fixed to keep dry.

It started to rain that night and just kept it up for days. I lost track of time, as each day was just like the one before.

I had nothing to read. I was just all alone and couldn't do anything without getting soaked. The roar of the river and wind through the timber just about drove me bugs, so I spent most of my time sleeping.

Finally, the weather broke and I got out. I spent several days trying to find the old Indian's half-moon lake, but it couldn't be spotted.

I did find, about two miles from camp and up the river about a mile, a lake shaped like the letter S. On the creek coming out from the lower end, I panned some pretty good color, but I figured it wasn't anything to get excited about.

Talk about dead country that sure is. There doesn't seem to be any life in there at all. You might spend all day in the timber without seeing a squirrel.

I was getting tired of beans, rice and bacon, so I made up my mind I would go over to a ridge about eight miles east of the S lake and get a few grouse, as I thought I could hear a few hooters up there.

I left the next morning, taking my rifle with me. When I came to the ridge, sure enough, there were a few grouse hooting. I shot two of them and had gotten them, when I bagged another one which fell down the ridge a hundred yards before it hung up.

While on my way down to pick it up, I found that piece of quartz. Up to that time I paid very little attention to what the country looked like, as it was heavily timbered and brushy.

The formation didn't show up and I had no tools with me to uncover it. The top of an old snag had broken off and fallen.

I scraped the moss and loose dirt off for a space of about eight feet, and eighteen or twenty feet long, uncovering this quartz ledge which is where I found this piece.

This ledge was worked smooth by a glacier at one time and I couldn't find anything with which to break off a piece, so I used the butt of my gun, ruining it for further use.

This didn't worry me because I knew there was no game in the country larger than a grouse and damned few of them.

My first thought was of the richness of the quartz and of you fellows and getting back to town to round you all up so we could get busy on it.

After looking it over and enjoying the feeling that I had made a rich find, I covered the ledge up again with moss, limbs and rotten chunk.

Finishing that job, I thought I would climb the ridge directly over the ledge and get my landmarks, so I could come back to it again or tell you where it was if anything should happen to me.

I climbed about six hundred feet above the ledge. I looked down and picked out a big tree with a bushy top, taller than the rest and about fifty feet to the right of the ledge.

Looking out over the top of this tree, I could see Frederick Sound, Cape of the Straight Light, and the point of Vanderput Spit (Point Vanderput). Turning a little to the left, I could see Sukhoi Island (Kodiak) from the mouth of Wrangell Narrows.

Satisfied with that, I turned half around and lying below me on the other side of the ridge was the half-moon lake the Indian told me about.

Right there, fellows, I got the scare of my life. I hope to God I never see or go through the likes of it again. Swarming up the ridge toward me from the lake were the most hideous creatures.

I couldn't call them anything but devils, as they were neither men nor monkeys, yet they looked like both. They were entirely sexless. Their bodies were covered with long course hair, except where the scabs and running sores had replaced it.

Each one seemed to be reaching out for me and striving to be the first to get me. The air was full of their cries and the stench from their sores and bodies made me faint.

I tried to use my broken gun on the first ones and then I threw it at them and turned and ran. God! How I did run. I could feel their hot breath on my back.

Their long claw-like fingers scraped my back. The smell from their steaming stinking bodies was making me sick. The noises they made, yelling, screaming and breathing drove me mad.

Reason left me. How I reached the canoe or how I hung on to that piece of quartz is a mystery to me.

When I came to, it was night and I was lying in the bottom of my canoe, drifting between Thomas Bay and Sukhoi Island. I was cold, hungry and crazy for a drink of water.

I started for Wrangle and here I am.
You no doubt think I'm crazy or lying.
All I can say is, there is the quartz.
Never let me hear the name of Thomas
Bay again, and for God's sake, help me
to get away tomorrow on that boat!

With that, Charlie passed out of our lives, said Harry.

Alaska's ancient Southeastern Tlingit Native Americans use koosh taa kaa. It means a hair-covered giant, not an otter or otterman. Journalist Steven Levi spelled the term Kushtacah, which is defined as a sasquatch-like being who lives in the woods, often in caves and rocky outcroppings.

Ancient Haida-Tlingit narrative say that the koosh taa kaa live deep in the woods or on unoccupied islands. The Kushtacah whistles through its teeth and imitates bird calls such as wood hens, grouse and other game birds.

They are said to be accurate marksmen with rocks, pinecones and often use small sturdy branches as lances.

Kushtacah are tall people, reaching seven feet tall. They are covered with hair.

Other prospectors who scouted the same area have been reported as suffering frightening experiences and to behave in a strange manner afterward.

Mysterious happenings occurred as late as 1925, when a farmer reported losing a dog in the hills. He found strange tracks with hind feet resembling a cross between a bear and a human footprint.

A trapper disappeared from the area. Searchers found his outfit and tracks but no trace of the man.

9

The World of the Hobo

A young hobo seeing the world.

Some very famous people have ridden the rails, adopting a hobo's life out of necessity as much as for wanderlust adventure.

Consider these names among those who rode the rails as hoboes: Western writer Louis L'Amour, T.V. host Art Linkletter, Oil billionaire H.L. Hunt, Journalist Eric Severeid, Supreme Court Justice William O. Douglas, and writer Jack London.

Riding the rails during the depression years of the 1930s wasn't a joyride. It is estimated that at least 6,500 hoboes were killed in one year either in accidents or by railroad "bulls", the brutal guards hired by the railroads.

A hobo couldn't just go to a railroad yard and climb on because of the alert railroad "bulls". A hobo had to run along the train as it gained speed, grab hold and jump into open boxcars.

If they missed, they risked losing their legs or even their lives. As a train neared its destination, the hoboes were forced to jump from the trains before a new set of railroad bulls spotted them.

A hobo is a migratory worker or homeless vagabond—especially one who is penniless. The term originated in the West—probably Northwestern—United States around 1890. Unlike "tramps" who work only when they are forced to, and "bums" who do not work at all, hobos are itinerant workers.

Walter Ballard was a hobo during the depression years. He remembers that times were so bad that his family didn't have enough to eat. Ballard recalled that in Chadron, Nebraska, there were so many hoboes on the train that the brakeman gave up trying to control them.

"There were so many people on it, it looked like blackbirds."

Even considering all the danger, Ballard liked the hobo life.

"I loved it," he said. "It'll get in your blood. You're not going anywhere, you don't care, and you just ride. It's paid for."

Hopping a moving freight car could be dangerous business.

One of the first hoboes (often called "tramps") to write about the hobo life was Josiah Flynt. His published articles in the 1890s describing tramp life abroad, at home, and on the rails, caused the railroad companies to hire him as an informant.

It is believed that ten thousand hoboes are enjoying free transportation between railroad towns each night.

Choosing where to ride was always a consideration. Where the hobo ended up riding depended on the type of train and the obstacles on that train, especially the railroad bulls.

"Riding the blinds" meant to ride the front platform of the baggage car on a passenger train.

Because baggage was piled up inside, thus blocking the doors between cars, it was a relatively secure place to sit. However, it also made a rider an easy target for water hoses or showers of hot coal or hot ash from sadistic firemen.

Empty boxcars, or even those lightly loaded, were popular traveling spots for hoboes. Some hoboes even lit fires in freezing box cars to stay warm.

Refrigerator cars could be dangerous places to ride. Hostile railroad bulls were known to lock the "reefer" doors from the outside, trapping trespassers inside to freeze to death.

Some of the more knowledgeable hoboes might carry a piece of wood with them to keep the door from locking shut.

It is believed that from 1901 to 1903, as many as 25,000 hoboes trespassing on the rail trains were killed. An equal number were maimed and crippled.

"The Famous Tramp", or Number 1, was a tramp who traveled 500,000 miles for $7.61.

Not an unusual sighting on a rail track.

The train riders had their own jargon. Consider the following:

- Sticks: A train rider who lost a leg.
- Peg: A train rider who lost a foot.
- Fingy or fingers: a rider who lost one or more fingers.
- Blinky: A trainer rider who lost one or both eyes.

- Mitts: A train rider who lost one or both hands.
- Righty: a rider who lost his right arm and leg.
- Lefty: a rider who lost a left arm and a leg.
- Halfy: A rider who lost both legs below the knees.
- Straight Crip: a rider who was crippled or otherwise afflicted.
- Phoney Crip: Self-mutilated or simulating deformity.

It's unclear when the first hobos appeared on the American railroad scene. At the end of the American Civil War in the 1860s, many discharged veterans returning home began hopping freight trains.

Hobo conventions are held throughout the country, often as part of "Railroad Days" The most notable hobo convention is the National Hobo Convention held in Britt, Iowa. It's been held on the second weekend in August since 1934.

The hobo culture developed a long list of expressions that describe the hobo life. Consider the following:

- Accommodation Car: The railroad caboose.
- Angellina: A young inexperienced child.
- Bad Road: A train rendered useless by some hobo's bad action or crime.
- Banjo: A small portable frying pan.

- Barnacle: A person who sticks to one job for a year or more.
- Beachcomber: a hobo who hangs around docks and seaports.
- Big House: Prison
- Bindle stick: A collection of belongings wrapped in cloth and tied around a stick.
- Blowed in the glass: a genuine trustworthy fellow.
- Boil up: To boil ones clothes to kill lice and their eggs. Generally to get oneself as clean as possible.
- Bone polisher: a mean dog.
- Bull: A railroad officer.
- Bullets: beans
- Buck: a Catholic priest good for a dollar.
- California blankets: Newspapers for bedding.
- Cannonball: a fast train.
- Catch the Westbound: To die.
- Chuck a dummy: Pretend to faint.
- Cover with the moon: Sleep in the open.
- Cow crate: A railroad stock car.
- Crumbs: Lice
- Doggin' it: Traveling by Greyhound bus.
- Elevated: Under the influence of drugs or alcohol.
- Flip: To board a moving train.
- Graybacks: Lice
- Grease the track: Get run over by a train.
- Honey dipping: Working with a shovel in a sewer.
- Jungle: a hobo camp

■ Tokay blanket: drink alcohol to stay warm

A businessman that tried the hobo life told of a culinary learning experience. Three of us kids caught a freight train and got some 60 or 70 miles from home before nightfall.

We didn't know how to spend the night. Several attempts to quarter ourselves in empty box cars only resulted in our being chased away and threatened with arrest.

We went to the outskirts of town and built a fire on the bank of a creek. A hobo came along and asked if we had anything to eat. Of course we didn't.

"Well," he said, "if you fellers'll fetch me a chicken, I'll show you a trick that'll be useful to you."

"It didn't take long for us to catch a chicken and bring it back."

The hobo took the chicken and jerked its head off, cleaned it and went down to the creek. He wrapped it, feathers and all, in a ball of yellow clay. This he rolled into the fire and scraped the embers around it. The clay soon hardened and we could see gradually becoming a cherry red.

When it turned red, the hobo cook rolled it out of the coals and let it cool. He then broke the clay covering with a stone. The feathers stuck to the clay and the baked chicken came out clean and ready to serve.

10

Death of the Telegram

Samuel Morse

Without fanfare, Western Union just decided to call it a day. Of course, the telegram was 145 years old and had gotten a little tired and unwanted.

An early Samuel Morse telegraph machine.

During its active lifetime, Western Union certainly served a noble purpose. But in a sad way, one must remember that it was this same Western Union that put the Pony Express out of business.

The telegram changed the world when its first message was sent on May 24, 1844. That message was simple, proclaiming, "What has God wrought?"

Those were the words that Samuel Morse himself sent as a test message to his dedicated employee Mr. Watson.

Getting the public to believe in his new invention was a tougher chore than Morse anticipated. In the beginning, it was considered little more than a curiosity.

Morse was a professor of arts and design at New York University when he proved that signals could be transmitted by wire and produce written codes on a strip of paper. The year was 1835.

The next year, Morse modified the device to write dots and dashes. The public remained skeptical.

Samuel Morse explaining his telegraph machine to Congress.

Morse decided to seek help from the federal government. In 1837, he applied for government assistance in developing the telegraph. It was in this same year the nation suffered an economic disaster known as the Panic of 1837.

Nothing was done with Morse's application.

Undaunted, Morse began giving public demonstrations of his device and gaining credibility.

As the nation recovered from its 1837 collapse, Morse again went to Congress for help. He asked for an appropriation to help build a telegraph line from Washington to Baltimore, a distance of 40 miles.

This time, legislators were receptive to Morse's idea. They granted him $30,000 to build his telegraph line. In a partnership with several other men, Morse began the building of more and more telegraph lines, expanding the availability of the newfangled invention.

The government rejected Morse's proposal to buy Morse's invention outright. Expansion of the line fell solely on private enterprise.

Into this melee walked a company called "The New York and Mississippi Valley Printing Telegraph". This company was in the process of buying several rival companies and in 1856, changed their name to Western Union Telegraph Company.

Five years later, Western Union completed the first transcontinental telegraph line, putting the fledgling Pony Express out of business.

During the American Civil War, the coast-to-coast communication system played a vital role.

Morse had an early career as an accomplished painter. He traveled to England in 1811 to study painting. After returning to the United States, he received commissions to paint former Presidents John Adams and James Monroe.

By 1856, there were thirty to forty rival companies working on different patents of the telegraph.

Samuel Morse's painting of John Adams. He also painted a portrait of President James Monroe.

Other technology then came into existence, including the telephone. Long distance telephone service was an expensive service and telegrams peaked during the 1920s and 1930s. It was cheaper to send a telegram than to place a long-distance telephone call.

During World War II, the appearance of a Western Union courier was not a welcome sight. The War Department used Western Union to notify families of the deaths and injuries of armed forces personnel.

As technology improved, the telegram was doomed. Faxes, emails and cheaper long distance rates simply overpowered the telegram.

A Pony Express rider gallops by as workmen install telegraph poles in the early engraving.

No less than Thomas Edison served as a telegraph operator. Edison saved three-year-old Jimmie MacKenzie from being struck by a runaway train.

The boy's father, J.U. MacKenzie, was a station agent in Mount Clemens, Michigan. He was so grateful to Edison that he trained him as a telegraph operator.

In 1866, at age 19, Edison moved to Louisville, Kentucky, where, as an employee of Western Union, he worked the Associated Press bureau news wire.

He requested the night shift, which gave him plenty of time to spend at his two favorite pastimes—reading and experimenting. His experimenting hobby cost him his Western Union job.

One night, in 1867, Edison was working with a lead-acid battery when he spilled sulfuric acid onto the floor. It ran between the floorboards and onto his boss's desk below. The next morning Edison was fired.

11

Galveston, Texas Hurricane Kills 6,000

Galveston's 1900 hurricane took between 6,000 and 12,000 lives.

The deadliest storm in U.S. history hit Galveston, Texas on September 8, 1900. Winds raged at 145 miles per hour.

Galveston Island is one-and-a-half miles wide and 27 miles long. The first European to see the island was probably Spanish explorer Alonzo Alvarez de Pineda.

It is believed that when Cabeza de Vaca was shipwrecked on a Gulf island that he called Isla de Malhado (Island of Misfortune) in 1528, he may have been on Galveston Island.

Hurricanes struck Galveston 11 times during the 19th century. In 1818, the entire island was flooded to a depth of four feet, leaving only six buildings habitable.

After the storm of 1837, a local carpenter, Joseph Ehlinger, suggested rebuilding the destroyed customs-house on four-foot pilings. This would raise it about the flood level.

Since that time, many structures, residences included, were built on stilts.

On the Saturday morning before the hurricane hit Galveston, rain clouds were building up and the tide was higher than usual.

The rain gauge blew down from its perch atop the Levy Building at 2:30 p.m. At 5:15, the anemometer blew away. Storm survivors told of seeing slate, timbers, bricks and other heavy debris being blown through the air horizontally.

The storm made matchsticks out of frame buildings. Even buildings built to withstand strong winds were battered apart by floating bridge trestles. Collapsing buildings caught and held victims under water.

Galveston's entire island was covered by a storm surge of 15.7 feet of water. The wind and rain stopped and the water receded, but bodies lay everywhere.

The flood waters reached waist deep in Galveston.

Many victims were buried in huge piles of rubble that covered the city. They were discovered only as clean-up progressed. Structures in two-thirds of the city were totally destroyed.

Officials said there would probably never be a full accounting of all the people who perished in the 1900 storm.

The most urgent task in the semi-tropical climate was to dispose of the remains of victims for health reasons. The powerful stench of decaying bodies forced searchers to wear handkerchiefs saturated with camphor over their noses.

Many drank whiskey to dull the horror. When not enough volunteers could be found to perform the grizzly task, men were rounded up at gunpoint or bayonet point to do it.

Men tug at ropes to remove debris from flood victims.

At first, the remains were transported on barges, weighted down with heavy rocks and dumped into the sea. Some of the bodies began to float ashore. Instead of dumping them at sea, rescuers used funeral pyres to cremate the victims.

The funeral pyres burned until November. About 70 victims a day were found during the first month following the storm. It wasn't until February 10, 1901 that the last body was found.

Besides the human toll, an estimated property damage, including 3,600 homes destroyed, amounted $30 million. The wagon bridge washed away, leaving railroads as the only transportation to the mainland.

Red Cross workers plant 1.5 million strawberry plants Clara Barton ordered for the devastated Galveston area.

Clara Barton, the 78-year-old founder of the **American Red Cross**, arrived on September 17 with a group of workers. Barton brought in 1.5 million strawberry plants that workers planted.

The Central Relief Committee delegated the distribution of food and clothing to the Red Cross. Donations poured in from cities throughout the United 'States and from several foreign countries.

Money came from millionaires, from black churches in Georgia, and from a little girl in Chicago who sent 10 cents. In all, donations exceeded $1.25 million.

A commission was appointed to help Galveston recover. Galveston kept the commission form of city government until 1960. Engineers presented a two-part project.

To break the force of the waves, a concrete wall three miles long was proposed. The commission also proposed raising the level of the entire city by picking up most of the structures in the city and filling in beneath them with sand.

A 17-foot sea wall now protects the city of Galveston.

A seawall was built in 50-foot sections. Piles were driven 40 to 50 feet deep and set four feet apart. A construction crew poured about 100 feet of seawall per day.

When the seawall was finished, it stood 17-feet above the mean low tide. All buildings that weren't already on stilts—about 2,000 buildings—were raised with jacks. Even the 3,000-foot St. Patrick's Church was lifted five feet with 700 jackscrews.

The sand for the fill was dredged out of an area between jetties at the entrance of Galveston Harbor. To transport the sand to the areas being raised, the contractor build a canal 20 feet deep, 200 feet wide and two-and-a-half miles long through the residential district.

A side benefit of the grade raising was that the city's sewer system, which never worked right, now had enough slope to operate properly. When the job was finished in 1910, 500 city blocks had been raised from a few inches to more than 16 feet.

12

Yuma Territorial Prison

Yuma Territorial Prison was built in 1875. For the next 33 years, it housed 3,069 prisoners.

Yuma Territorial Prison held both male and female inmates. For more than three decades, the prison was home to convicts from 21 different countries. They included prostitutes, carpenters, cooks, farmers, gamblers, wheelwrights, sailors and laborers.

Their crimes included murder, polygamy, adultery and theft. The convicts faced sizzling summers and cold winters in their cells.

When they tried to escape, they were fitted with a ball and chain. If they repeatedly tried to escape, they were thrown in a dark cell nicknamed the "snake den".

The dark cell was a room about 10 feet by 10 feet. It contained an iron cage in which the prisoners would be locked. The only light for the cell came from a small ventilation shaft in the ceiling. Contact with other people was forbidden.

Female outlaw Pearl Hart was one notable assigned to Yuma Territorial Prison.

At age 17, she was seduced by gambler Frederick Hart. She eloped with him but the marriage endured one hardship after another.

Pearl left her husband and moved to Colorado where she gave birth to their child. She then returned home in Ontario, Canada and left her son in the care of her mother.

To survive, Pearl returned to Phoenix. Fred Hart returned, begging her to take him in. Hart worked as a bartender and as a hotel manager. For three years there was peace in the Hart family.

In 1898, Hart told Pearl he was tired of supporting her and their child. A fight ensued and Frederick Hart knocked Pearl unconscious and left. He joined the army and left to fight the Spanish in Cuba with Teddy Roosevelt's Rough Riders.

Pearl took her second child to Ontario, Canada to deposit it with her mother and then drifted back to Arizona.

She worked in a number of hellhole mining comps as a cook before taking up with a carefree prospector named Joe Boot.

Pearl then received a letter from her brother telling her that her mother was ill and needed money for medical attention.

Joe Boot hit on a means for them to get some money. They would rob the stagecoach running from Globe to Florence, Arizona.

Since nobody had robbed a stagecoach in years, this coach did not have a shotgun rider. This stagecoach was one of the last to run in Arizona Territory.

Pearl armed herself with a Colt .44 and Joe Boot took a shotgun. As the stagecoach appeared, they jumped out in the road, ordered the driver to halt. As Boot held his shotgun on the driver, Pearl collected valuables and money from the passengers.

Pearl and Boot then rode their horses into the hills. They got lost and wandered through the hills for several days. They fell asleep next to a large campfire.

They were roused by a sheriff's posse and put under arrest.

As a woman, Pearl was something of a curiosity as she strutted behind the bars of her cell, playing the part of a desperado. She was tried twice in Florence, Arizona and sentenced to five years at Yuma Territorial Prison.

Joe Boot, in a separate trial, was sentenced to thirty years in the same prison.

The warden at the prison had to prepare a separate cell for Pearl, separating her from the all-male population. Pearl became a pest to the other prisoners by preaching gospel messages. One prisoner said, "She drove us nuts. We begged the warden to get rid of this woman."

She was released by Governor A.W. Brodie eighteen months later on the grounds that the prison had no accommodations for women.

William Jordan Flake

Then there was Mormon prisoner William Jordan Flake. The newly-formed Republican Party linked slavery and polygamy as the "twin relics of barbarism". They supported the Morrill Anti-Bigamy Act in 1862.

In 1882, Senator George F. Edmunds, of Vermont, sponsored the Edmunds Act, which made "unlawful cohabitation" a felony. Nine Mormon leaders were imprisoned in Yuma Territorial Prison under the provisions of the act.

William Jordan Flake was sent to the Yuma Territorial Prison in 1877. He was arrested for having a "plural marriage". Many Mormons fled to Mexico to avoid prosecution.

Flake decided to challenge the Edmund Act, calling it a mockery, a travesty of justice. He served six months in prison. He then lived out his days as a respected community leader and a cattleman in Snowflake, Arizona with his two wives, Prudence and Lucy, and their twenty children.

Mormon prisoners convicted on federal charges presented a difficult challenge for Superintendent Frank Ingalls. These new convicts were completely different from the murderers, rapists, embezzlers and other lawless convicts who populated the prison.

In 1890, the LDS Church issued the Manifesto, which banned plural marriage. One can still ask the question, were these men jailed for breaking the law or for their religious beliefs?

Ironically, the prison had more amenities than most of the homes in Yuma. Many residents resented that.

The prison had electricity, forced ventilation, sanitation (including bathtubs and three showers), a library with 2,000 books, and even a prison band. It was sometimes referred to as the "Country Club on the Colorado".

Still, prisoners feared and loathed the Territorial Prison.

The heat was insufferable; it was surrounded by rivers, quick sand and desert in all directions. The inhuman "Snake Den" and "Ball and Chain" were detested punishments. Tuberculosis was a killer and the prison was impossible to escape.

13

Oscar the Therapy Cat

Oscar the therapy cat.

Oscar was adopted as a kitten from an animal shelter by the Steere House Nursing and Rehabilitation Center Providence, Rhode Island.

The 41-bed unit treats people with Alzheimer's, Parkinson's and other illnesses, most of which are the end state of life. Most of the patients are unaware of their surroundings.

Oscar had the uncanny ability to predict when a patient was going to die.

It was a nurse named Mary that first noticed Oscar's unusual ability. She became aware that the cat only spent time with patients who were about to die. Some family members believe differently, saying that Oscar is not there for the dying but for the living.

Dr. David Dosa wrote about Oscar in a book, "Making the Rounds with Oscar".

Since ancient times, animals have shown an ability to predict the future. It is no secret that they can feel when a natural disaster is coming. Cats, researchers say, are the most likely to predict a misfortune.

Oscar, who lived on the roof of the mental hospital in Rhode Island, proved he could predict death of terminally ill patients. About two hours before a patient breathed their last gasp, Oscar would snuggle down on the patient's beds.

At two years old, Oscar predicted correctly the death of more than 100 patients. The staff learned to trust Oscar's intuition completely. When Oscar climbed onto a patient's bed, the staff knew it was time to call the patient's family members.

Specialists have two explanations for Oscar's sixth sense. They believe his ability to predict death may be connected with the fact that most patients can't move or that Oscar is able to smell ketones. Ketones are biochemicals released by dying cells.

Oscar was adopted along with five other kittens by the mental facility after the Steere House's first therapy pet died. While Oscar may snuggle up to terminal patients, he is not all friendly with other patients.

Dr. Joan Teno, a professor of community health at Warren Alpert Medical School of Brown University, cares for patients at Steere House. She comes into contact with Oscar on a regular basis.

"Oscar doesn't make too many mistakes. It's not that the cat is consistently there first. He seems to understand when patients are about to die. It seems he always manages to make an appearance, and that always seems to be in the last two hours."

If Oscar is made to stay in the hallway outside the room of a dying patient, he gets quite upset and starts to do laps outside the door, whining.

Dr. Dosa, an assistant professor of medicine at Brown University, said "I never intended to make Oscar sound creepy or his arrival at bedside to be viewed negatively."

Dr. Margie Scherk, a veterinarian in Vancouver, British Columbia, said, "Cats can smell a lot of things that we can't. And cats can certainly detect illness."

Dr. Jill Goldman, a certified animal behaviorist in Laguna Beach, California, said, Cats have a superb sense of smell. There has been ample opportunity for Oscar to make an association between the smell of death and mere illness. He has spent nearly his entire life in the end-stage dementia unit of Steere House where death is common and expected.

Dosa recalls one instance when the staff was convinced of the imminent death of one patient but Oscar refused to sit with that person. He chose instead the bed of another patient a ways down the hallway.

Oscar proved to be right. The patient with whom Oscar sat died first.

"The first time I met Oscar, he bit me," said Dr. Dosa. "We have warmed over the years. I don't think Oscar is that unique, but he is in a unique environment. Animals are remarkable in their ability to see things that we don't, be it the dog that sniffs cancer or the fish that predicts earthquakes. Animals know when they are needed."

Dosa said it's not like Oscar just dawdles. He'll slip out of room and grab some kibble and then he's back at the patient's side. It's like he's literally on a vigil."

The nursing home keeps five other cats but none these has ever displayed a similar ability.

Not everyone agrees that Oscar's abilities are unique. Skeptics have classed Oscar's alleged abilities as pseudoscientific. They suggest more attention should be paid to Dr. Ray Hyman's "Categorical Imperative", which says, "Do not try to explain something until you are sure there is something to be explained."

14

Boston Corbett
'He castrated himself with scissors'

Boston Corbett

He was known as the man who killed John Wilkes Booth, President Abraham Lincoln's assassinator.

Thomas H. Corbett was born in London, England, in 1832. He came to New York in 1839.

Corbett became a hatter in Troy, New York. He later moved to Boston where he continued working as a hatter. He married, but his wife died in childbirth.

It is known that Corbett had mental problems. It is believed the problems were caused by his frequent association with mercury used in the hatter's trade.

Corbett was a re-born evangelical Christian. Reform became his purpose in life. He tried to imitate Jesus. He thus wore his hair very long. People who knew him said he was "different".

At the outbreak of the Civil War, Corbett eagerly joined the Union Army. He was in hot water from the first day he joined. He became the regiment's self-appointed moral guardian.

During a review, when the colonel roundly cursed the men as they stood at attention, Corbett stepped out of ranks to reprimand the commanding officer. He spent some time in the guardhouse after that.

Another infraction nearly got him executed. When he abandoned his post one night, insisting that his enlistment was up at midnight, the army disagreed.

Corbett was arrested, tried and convicted and sentenced to be shot. For a time, his life hung in the balance. In the end, the Army simply expelled him.

He didn't stay a civilian for very long. He enlisted in the 16th New York Cavalry and became a sergeant. Corbett got his real chance at combat when his unit had a brush with Confederate raiders under John Singleton Mosby.

Cut off from his comrades, Corbett continued to fight against the great odds. True to form, he would shout, "Amen! Glory to God!" each time his bullets found their mark.

He killed seven enemies before he ran out of ammunition. Only then did he surrender. He was sent to Andersonville Prison in Georgia. He was reduced to a near skeleton before being released.

On October 24, 1865, he was selected as one of the 26 cavalry men to pursue John Wilkes Booth, the killer of Abraham Lincoln.

Booth was cornered in a tobacco barn on the Virginia farm of Richard Garrett. His accomplice, David Herold, had surrendered to troopers of the 16th New York Cavalry.

As booth moved around inside the barn, Corbett shot him with a Colt revolver from a distance of no more than 12 feet. He explained his actions by saying, "Providence directed my hand."

Booth's body was dragged from the barn and he died a few hours later. His spinal cord had been punctured by Corbett's bullet.

Corbett was placed under technical arrest but the charges were dropped by Secretary of War Edmond M. Stanton, who said, "The rebel is dead. The patriot lives."

Corbett's steady aim earned him certain celebrity. He was the man who rid the world of Lincoln's assassin. People soon began to notice something strange about Boston Corbett.

Instead of signing his name when asked for an autograph, he would pen lengthy passages about the Almighty.

John Wilkes Booth, Lincoln's assassin.

His strange behavior became more noticeable when he discovered the downside of his celebrity. Crank letters began arriving. The volume of hate mail increased, some accompanied by death threats.

Corbett's fears blossomed into paranoia. He took to pointing his gun at autograph seekers.

The hatter's zeal reached new heights on the night of July 16, 1858. After he spied two prostitutes walking down the street, they inspired lust in him. He returned home and read Mark 19:12, which quote Christ as saying, "they have made themselves eunuchs for the Kingdom of God's sake.

Corbett took a pair of scissors and castrated himself. He calmly cut an opening in his scrotum, pulled out the testes and cut them off. After castrating himself, he went to a prayer meeting and ate a full dinner. He then took a walk, but eventually went to see a doctor.

He ended up in Massachusetts General Hospital and was treated by Dr. R.N. Hodges. The hospital record of Corbett's self-castration and treatment still exists.

Corbett received a share of the reward money, which amounted to $1,653.85.

After the war, Corbett returned to being a hatter. In 1878, he moved to Concordia, Kansas.

He filed a claim on 80 acres seven miles south of town. There he lived in a dugout. Corbett slept on a homemade bed and kept a variety of firearms. He established a reputation as being a recluse.

He purchased a flock of sheep and won local respect for his ability to shoot crows and hawks. When word got out that he was a celebrity for shooting John Wilkes Booth, he was invited to give a speech on the Booth affair and on his days at Andersonville Prison.

Surprisingly, he accepted. When he showed up, however, he refused to say anything about Booth or Andersonville. Instead he began haranguing the crowd at length about the need to repent.

For the most part, he remained aloof from his neighbors. He hired four men to work on his farm. They planted some corn but Corbett himself never appeared in the fields until evening.

He soon gave up farming and began raising chickens and a few head of livestock. His source of funds became a curiosity of the locals. He paid cash for everything he bought, yet he never worked.

Corbett did have some contact with one neighbor, a Mrs. Randall, who sold him milk and butter. He confided to her that he wanted to be buried on his farm and showed her and another woman a grave he had dug near his dugout house.

There came about a somewhat violent incident that further isolated him from his neighbors. It took place one Sunday morning.

Corbett was reading scripture while driving pas a baseball game in his buckboard. He became incensed that the local boys were playing baseball on the Sabbath.

He stopped his horse, took a pistol from his belt and shouted, "It is wicked to play baseball on the Lord's Day!" As he brandished his weapons, the frightened youngsters and bystanders scattered.

The next day, a warrant was sworn out for his arrest. He was order to stand trial in the office of Concordia's Justice of the Peace. The whole town turned out to see the "entertainment".

Corbett showed up fully armed. At first he seemed calm, but as a series of witnesses testified about his violent outburst, he became grimmer.

When the adults who were spectators at the baseball game testified about his violent outburst, Corbett erupted in a torrent of vehement denials and pointing his pistol at the witnesses.

"That's a lie, lie, lie!" he shouted. "I'll shoot any man who says such things against me!"

Officials managed to calm Corbett, who left the office unmolested.

A well-meaning politician was able to get Corbett appointed assistant doorkeeper of the Kansas House of Representatives in Topeka. A for a month, all went well. Corbett stuck to his duties and became somewhat of a tourist attraction as the man who killed John Wilkes Booth.

But the hatter went off the rails again. He heard blasphemous remarks being made during a legislative session's opening prayer. Corbett started running around the corridors waving his pistol as legislators took cover.

No one was hurt, but Corbett was committed to the Topeka Asylum for the Insane.

15

Ada Lovelace
First Computer Expert

She was born in 1815, and was the world's first computer programmer. She was an English mathematician and writer and was chiefly known for her work on Charles Babbage's early general purpose computer.

She is recognized for writing the first algorithm intended to be carried by a machine.

Ada was the only child of the poet Lord Byron and his wife Anne Isabella Byron. All of Byron's other children were born out of wedlock to other women.

Byron separated from his wife a month after Ada was born. He left England forever four months later and died of disease in the Greek War of independence when Ada was eight years old.

Ada Lovelace

She was born Augusta Ada Byron, Countess of Lovelace. Ada's mother remained bitter towards Lord Byron and promoted Ada's interest in mathematics and logic. She wanted to prevent her from developing what she saw as the insanity seen in her father.

Ada, however, remained interested in Lord Byron despite her mother's bitterness.

As a young adult, Ada's mathematical talents led her to a working relationship with British mathematician Charles Babbage. Between 1842 and 1843, she translated an article by Italian military engineer Luigi Menabrea on the machine.

She supplemented the article was elaborate notes of her own. These notes contained what many consider to be the first computer program. She also developed a vision on the capability of computers to go beyond mere calculating or number-crunching.

Ada was ill throughout her early childhood. She was paralyzed after a bout with measles in 1829. She was subjected to bed rest for nearly a year. By 1831, she was able to walk on crutches.

Despite her illness, she developed her mathematical and technological skills. At age 12, she decided she wanted to fly. She went about the project methodically and thoughtfully.

Her first step was to construct wings. She considered various materials including paper, oil silk, wires and feathers. She examined the anatomy of birds to determine the right proportion between the wings and the body.

In 1833, she had an affair with a tutor. She was caught trying to elope with him. In 1835, Ada married William King, 8th Baron King. She thus became Lady Baroness King.

Early computing machines were called "Turing Machines". A Turing machine could do anything the most complicated computer can do if we ignore memory sizes and other modern computer capabilities.

Charles Babbage

Charles Babbage set out to build a machine that was capable of doing a variety of mathematical calculations correctly every time. He wanted to get rid of the errors that were inherent when humans did calculations by hand.

Babbage's earliest computers did not run on electricity. They were entirely mechanical. He did make some designs that were run with steam while others needed to be hand-cranked.

His first "Difference Machine" was made up of more than 25,000 parts. It weighed roughly fifteen tons. However, it was never completed in terms of construction as Babbage had designed it. It was only half built.

This engine was constructed by the Science Museum in London from designs made by the British computing pioneer Charles Babbage (1791-1871) between 1847 and 1849. The main part of the engine was completed in 1991 for the bicentennial year of Babbage's birth, and the printing mechanism was completed in 2000. Doron Swade, senior curator of computing and IT, is seen with it here in the Computing Gallery of the Science Museum. Babbage conceived the engine to calculate a series of numerical values and automatically print the results. Difference Engine No 2 was never constructed in his lifetime. Front view.

Charles Babbage constructed this "Difference Engine" between 1847 and 1849. Shown with the machine is Doron Swade, senior curator of computing and IT in the Computing Gallery of the Science Museum.

The difference Engine was capable of returning mathematical results up to 31 digits. Babbage failed to build a second machine due to funding problems. This machine he called "The Analytical Engine".

This machine would allow someone to make a program with "punch" cards once, and then be able to use the program over and over without having to manually redo everything every time.

The Analytical Machine could also use results of previous calculations in future calculations.

16

He Invented
The Stethoscope

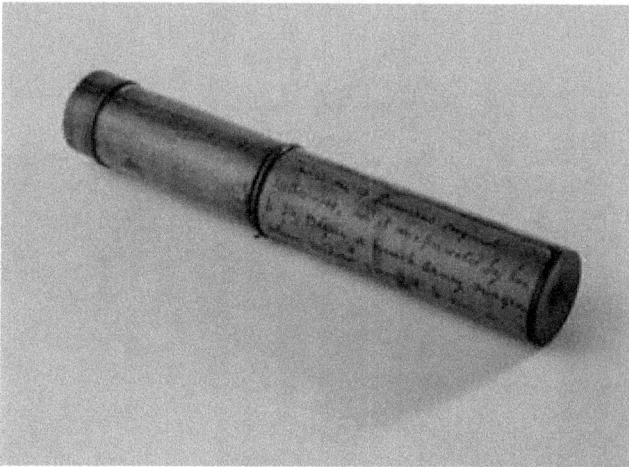

First stethoscope in 1822

Rene Laennec's first stethoscope looked more like a kid's whistle than a medical instrument. Laennec was a French physician who worked at "Hopital (sic) Necker" when he invented the stethoscope in 1816.

Laennec's mother died of tuberculosis when he was five or six years old. He went to live with his grand uncle the Abbe Laennec (a priest). He then went to his uncle, Guillaime-Francois Laennec, who worked in the faculty of medicine at the university.

Rene Laennec

Young Rene was a gifted student. He learned English and German and began medical studies under his uncle's direction.

His father, a lawyer, tried to discourage his son from continuing his medical studies. There was therefore a period of time when Rene took long walks in the country, danced, studied Greek and wrote poetry.

In 1779, he returned to his medical studies. He studied in Paris under several famous physicians, including Dupuytren and Jean-Nicolas Corvisart-Desmarets.

Rene had a patient who had a diseased heart but was too fat for him to properly diagnose.

He remembered a simple and well-known fact in acoustics: the great distinctness with which we hear the scratch of a pin at one end of a piece of wood while applying an ear to another.

Laennec rolled a quire of paper (about 25 sheets) into a cylinder and applied one end of it to the region of the heart and the other to his ear. He was not a little surprised to find he could hear the action of the heart in a much more clear and distinct manner.

He found this was much superior to simply placing an ear over the chest, particularly if the patient is overweight.

A stethoscope also avoids the embarrassment of placing an ear against the chest of a woman.

Rene built his first instrument from a 256 cm by 2.5 cm hollow wooden cylinder.

He wanted to name the device *le cylinder*, claiming it was frivolous to name such a device. His colleagues thought it should have a name. Rene rejected the names they came up with and decided to call it a stethoscope. Stethe comes from the Greek term for chest, and scope from the Latin term for aim.

His clinical studies allowed him to follow chest patients from bedside to the autopsy table. He could correlate sounds captured by the new instrument with specific pathological changes in the chest.

He coined the phrase *mediate auscultation* (indirect listening) as opposed to the practice of placing the ear directly on the chest.

Not all doctors readily embraced the new stethoscope.

Laennec was famous for other medical contributions as well. He developed the understanding of peritonitis and cirrhosis. Although the disease cirrhosis was known, Laennec gave cirrhosis its name.

He used the Greek word *kirrhos* (tawny) that referred to the yellow nodules characteristic of the disease.

Laennec coined the term melanoma and described metastases of melanoma to the lungs. In 1804, while still a medical student, he was the first person to lecture on melanoma.

He learned to recognize pneumonia, bronchiectasis, pleurisy, emphysema, and other lung diseases from the sounds he heard with his stethoscope.

Professor Benjamin Ward Richardson stated in *Disciples of Aesculapius* that "A true student of medicine reads Laennec's treatise on mediate auscultation and the use of the stethoscope every two years as long as he is in practice."

Laennec died from tuberculosis on August 13, 1826 at 45 years of age.

17

First Woman to Run
For U.S. President

Victoria

Woodhull

Few Americans recognize her name, but 150 years ago she was one of the best known women in America. Her name was Victoria Claflin Woodhull and she was the first woman to ever run for President.

She was also the first woman to open a bank on Wall Street.

Americans thrilled to the news stories about Victoria. They scooped up her books and pamphlets. Her lectures were spellbinding.

Woodhull maintained that a "Woman's ability to earn money is better protection against the tyranny and brutality than is her ability to vote."

Victoria and her sister, Tennessee Claflin, invaded Wall Street to achieve their economic independence. Newspapers hailed America's first female stockbrokers as "The Queens of Finance". Others called them "The Bewitching Sisters.

In her run for President, she had one good thing going for her. She had the silent backing of Cornelius Vanderbilt and his fortune.

Victoria Woodhull was born in Homer, Ohio in 1838 and was the mother of two children. She was 31 years old when she made her run for President.

Woodhull married Canning Woodhull at the age of 15. He was a doctor who turned out to be an alcoholic philanderer. To make matters worse, she gave birth to a mentally handicapped son in 1854.

She and her sister launched the Woodhull & Claflin's Weekly newspaper. The sixteen-page weekly claimed twenty-thousand subscribers and ran for six years.

The newspaper highlighted the lessons the women had learned on Wall Street. They were muckrakers at heart and published exposes on stock swindles, insurance frauds, and corrupt Congressional land deals.

Above all, the weekly addressed the issues that concerned women. It advanced the vision that women could live as men's equals in the work place, in the political arena, the church, the family circle and the bedroom.

VICTORIA C. WOODHULL and TENNIE C. CLAFLIN,

EDITORS AND PROPRIETORS.

All communications, business or editorial, must be addressed

Woodhull & Claflin's Weekly,

44 Broad Street, New York City.

Masthead of the Woodhull and Claflin Weekly had sixteen thousand subscribers.

Woodhull's experience as a lobbyist and businesswoman taught her how to penetrate the all-male domain of national politics. In one instance, she pre-empted the opening of the 1871 National Woman's Suffrage Associations convention.

Suffrage leaders postponed their meeting to listen to Woodhull address the House Judiciary Committee.

She argued that women already had the right to vote. All they had to do was use it.

In the election, Woodhull challenged incumbent Ulysses S. Grant and his Democratic opponent Horace Greeley. The Equal Rights Party selected her as their standard bearer six months after Woodhull delivered her first social freedom speech.

In an ironic twist of fate, Victoria Woodhull spent Election Eve behind bars. Woodhull and Claflin were arrested for using the U.S. mails to "utter obscene publication" for taking to task Luther Challis, a stockbroker who boasted about his conquests of innocent young girls.

The so-called "Queens of the Quill" spent weeks in various New York City jails, paid bail—more than $60,000—for alleged misdemeanors. The sisters were found innocent of the obscenity counts in 1873 and innocent of libel in the Challis article in 1874.

On the lecture circuit, Woodhull spoke openly about sex, saying that women should have the right to escape bad marriages and control their own bodies.

She shocked Victorian sensibilities when she espoused free love. "I want the love of you all, promiscuously," she once exclaimed. "It makes no difference who or what you are, old or young, black or white, pagan, Jew or Christian, I want to love you all and be loved by you all."

She practiced what she preached. At one time, she lived with her ex-husband, her husband and her lover in the same apartment, all at the same time.

She said, "Let women issue a declaration of independence sexually, and absolutely refuse to cohabit with men until they are acknowledged as equals in everything. Victory would be won in a single week."

Victoria Woodhull apparently fared poorly in the election as none of the results that were posted showed her name and the number of votes she received.

18

He Invented Alternating Electrical Current

Nikola Tesla

Nikola Tesla received short shrift for his many inventions, including the design of alternating current in electricity.

Tesla gained experience in telephony and electrical engineering before immigrating to the United States in 1884 to work for Thomas Edison.

Tesla was soon able to venture out on his own after securing financial backing. He set up laboratories and companies to develop a wide range of electrical devices.

His patented AC induction motor and transformer were licensed by George Westinghouse. Westinghouse also hired Tesla for a time as a consultant.

Tesla pursued his ideas of wireless lighting and electricity distribution in his high voltage, high-frequency experiments in New York and Colorado Springs.

In 1893, he was working on the possibility of wireless communication with his devices. In his labs, Tesla conducted a range of experiments with mechanical oscillators/generators, electrical discharge tubes, and early X-ray imaging.

Tesla even built a wireless controlled boat, one of the first ever exhibited.

His patents earned him a considerable amount of money, most of which was used to financed his own projects.

Sometimes dubbed "The Mad Scientist", Tesla lived most of his life in a series of New York hotels.

Tesla was the fourth of five children. His mother Duka Tesla, had a talent for making home craft tools, mechanical appliances and the ability to memorize Serbian epic poems.

Nikola credited his eidetic memory and creative abilities to his mother's genetics and influence.

In 1882, he began working for Continental Edison Company in France, designing and making improvements to electrical equipment. In 1884, Thomas Edison hired Tesla and he relocated to New York.

His work for Edison began with simple electrical engineering and then progressed to solving difficult problems. He was offered the task of completely redesigning the Edison Company's direct current generators.

Tesla pointed out the inefficiency of Edison's direct current electrical powerhouses that were built up and down the Atlantic seaboard. He felt that alternating current would be more efficient because to him, all energies were cyclic.

He suggested that Edison build generators that would send electrical energy along distribution lines first one way and then another, in multiple waves using the polyphase principle.

In 1885, he said he could redesign Edison Company's direct current generators, making an improvement in both service and economy. Edison remarked, "There's $50,000 in it for you—if you can do it."

After months of work, Tesla fulfilled the task. He then asked about the payment. Edison replied that he was only joking, adding, "Tesla, you don't understand our American humor."

Edison Company offered him a $10 a week raise to go with his $18 a week salary. Tesla refused the offer and resigned.

He then partnered with two businessmen, Robert Lane and Benjamin Vale. The men agreed to finance an electric lighting company in Tesla's name. It would be called Tesla Electric Light & Manufacturing.

The company installed electrical arc light based illumination systems designed by Tesla. They also installed dynamo electric machine commutators, the first patents issued to Tesla in the U.S.

Lane and Vale eventually forced Tesla out of the company, leaving him penniless. Tesla even lost control of the patents he had generated since he had assigned them to the company in lieu of stock.

Tesla worked at various electrical repair jobs, and once even as a ditch-digger for $2 per day.

He was a lifelong bachelor and led a somewhat isolated existence. He devoted his full energies to science.

Some people speculated that Tesla was asexual and simply didn't have the urge towards sex. He did have this to say about women:

I put women on a lofty pedestal...I worshiped at the feet of the creature I had raised to this height, and like every true worshiper, and I felt myself unworthy of the object of my worship.

Tesla's concept of wireless electricity was used to power ocean liners, destroy warships, run industry and transportation and send communications instantaneously all over the globe.

According to Life Magazine's special issue of September 1997, Tesla was among the 100 most famous people of the last 1,000 years.

In 1915, a New York Times article announced that Tesla and Edison were to share the Nobel

Prize for physics. Oddly, neither man received the prize, the reason being unclear.

It was speculated that Tesla refused to share the award with Edison.

Tesla died January 7, 1943 in the Hotel New Yorker, where he had lived for the last 10 years, He was born in 1856.

19

Government Poisoned Alcohol During Prohibition

Government workers dump beer during Prohibition.

On Christmas Eve in New York City, a man afraid of Santa Claus stumbled into the emergency room at New York City's Bellevue Hospital.

Before the hospital staff realized how sick he was, he died.

Another party-goer also died, and another until the hospital staff racked up a total of 60 people who were made desperately ill by alcohol. Eight were dead from it.

It was a dark but little-known chapter of U.S. history. The federal government had ordered the poisoning of industrial alcohol used in paints, solvents, fuels and medicine to prevent their use in liquor sold to the public.

During the administration of President Calvin Coolidge, the alcohol industry was ordered to add higher levels of difficult to remove poisons to their alcohol. These poisons included acetone, benzene, cadmium, camphor, carbolic acid, cholorform, ether, formaldehyde, gasoline, iodine, kerosene, methyl alcohol, mercury salts, nicotine, quinine and zinc.

The poisoning program was no secret as the government hoped that knowledge of it would deter people from drinking, although alcohol consumption was not illegal.

Instead of deterring people from drinking, by the end of the Prohibition period in 1933, at least 10,000 people died from alcohol poisoning.

The incident is virtually forgotten today, but the government's "Chemist War of Prohibition" remains one of the strangest and most deadly decisions in American law enforcement history.

Charles Norris, the chief medical examiner for New York City during the 1920s, said, "It was our national experiment in extermination."

The government apparently didn't realize that poisoning industrial alcohol would cause such problems. While they wanted to scare people into giving up illicit drinking, they didn't realize that bootleggers would use the poisoned alcohol in their mixtures.

A product called Jamaica Ginger Extract, also known as "Jake", was sold in pharmacies during Prohibition. It contained alcohol so people used it as a substitute for liquor.

The government then required it to be "adulterated".

Two men who produced some of the extract found a way to trick the government adulteration test while retaining the extract's intoxicating effect.

The problem was their adulterant was a neurotoxin, and many people were paralyzed who drank it.

In 1930, large numbers of Jake users began to lose control over their hands and feet.

During Prohibition, the government's official sense of higher purpose kept the poisoning program in place.

The Chicago Tribune editorialized in 1927: "Normally, no American government would engage in such business. It is only in the curious fanaticism of Prohibition that any means, however barbarous, are considered justified."

There were some who approved of the government's alcohol poisoning program. Some argued that lawmakers opposed to the poisoning plan were in cahoots with criminals and those bootleggers and their law-breaking customers deserved no sympathy.

The Nebraska Omaha Bee asked, "Must Uncle Sam guarantee safety first for souses?"

The government's program started with the ratification of the 18th Amendment. This law banned the manufacture, sale or transportation of alcoholic beverages in the United States.

Despite the law, people continued to drink alcohol and to drink it in large quantities. Alcoholism rates actually soared during the 1920s. Insurance companies charted the increase at more than 300 percent.

During this period, speakeasies promptly opened for business. By the end of the decade, New York City alone had some 30,000 such places.

Street gangs grew into bootlegging empires built on smuggling, stealing, and manufacturing illegal alcohol.

Those who thought the 18th Amendment would usher in an era of upright behavior were shocked at what was happening.

The denaturing of alcohol didn't end until the 18th Amendment was repealed in 1933. But even before then, government officials quit talking about it. When Prohibition ended and good grain whiskey reappeared, it was almost as if the craziness of Prohibition had never happened.

20

Nat Love
The Life of a Black Cowboy

Nat Love, a black cowboy.

Nat Love was born a slave on the plantation of Robert Love in Davidson County, Tennessee. He figures the year was about 1854. "The exact date of my birth I never knew because in those days no count was kept of such trivial matters as the birth of a slave baby. They were born and died and the account was balanced on the gains and losses of the Master's chattels. One more or less did not matter."

Despite slavery laws that forbid black literacy, Nat (pronounced Nate) learned to read and write as a child with the help of his father, Sampson.

"My father was a sort of foreman of the slaves on the plantation, and my mother presided over the kitchen at the big house. Among her other duties was to milk the cows and run the loom, weaving clothing for the other slaves."

Young Nat witnessed the beatings given slaves who failed to meet the wishes of the men who owned them. "I have seen the long, cruel lash curl around the shoulders of women who refused to comply with the licentious wishes of the men who owned them."

Of all the curses of the slaves, Nat said, "The greatest curse of all was the slave auction block of the south, where human flesh was bought and sold. Husbands were torn from their wives, and the baby from its mother's breast."

Nat said that his family was lucky in this respect as his owner was kind and indulgent.

When Nat was 10-years-old, the American Civil War began. "There was little else talked about among the slaves as well as the slave owners. The many different stories we heard worked us children into a state of excitement. We wanted to war and to fight for the Union."

When Sampson Love died, young Nat took odd jobs to help make ends meet for his family. One day, he won a horse in a raffle. He promptly sold the horse to get enough money to leave town.

He traveled west to Dodge City, Kansas. He approached a group of cowboys who had driven a herd of Texas Longhorns up from Texas. Nat asked the foreman if he would hire him as a cowboy.

The boss agreed that Nat could join them if he could break a horse named "Good Eye". This was the wildest horse in the outfit and the Texas cowboys were sure they would have some fun watching this ride.

Bronco Jim, another black cowboy, gave Nat some pointers. Nat rode that horse to a standstill, winning the admiration of the entire group of cowboys. He said later, "It was the toughest ride I've ever had."

The trail driver gave him the promised job. The Duval Ranch cowboys gave him the name, "Red River Dick".

Nat had found his calling. He fought cattle rustlers, endured inclement weather, and was an excellent marksman.

While rounding up stray cattle near the Gila River in Arizona, Nat was captured by a band of Akimel O'odham (Pima) Indians. Nat claimed his life was spared because the Indians respected his fighting ability. He managed to steal a pony and escaped into west Texas.

Nat left the Texas Panhandle and rode into Arizona. There he got a job working for a cattle outfit on the Gila River. He found himself working with Mexican vaqueros. He learned to speak

Spanish like a native and became good at reading brands.

His outfit received an order to deliver three thousand head of the steers to Deadwood City in Dakota Territory. When they arrived, the town was getting ready for the 4th of July.

The mining men and gamblers organized a contest with $200 in prize money. Nat recalled that six of the dozen men in the contest were black. Each cowboy was to rope, throw, tie bridles, and saddle a mustang in the shortest time.

The wildest horses were chosen for the event. Nat roped, threw, tied bridles, saddled, and mounted his mustang in exactly nine minutes. The competitor closest to him clocked twelve minutes and thirty seconds.

In the rifle and Colt events, shooting at 100 and 250 yards with 14 shots, Nat placed all of his rifle shots inside the bull's eye and 10 of the 12 pistol shots in the bull's eye.

Along with the prize money the town gave Nat the name of "Deadwood Dick".

In 1889, Nat Love married a woman named Alice. The couple had one child. Nat then retired from the cowboy life. He took a job as a porter on a Pullman sleeping car.

His last job was as a security guard with the General Securities Company in Los Angeles. He died there in 1921.

21

Christopher Columbus Fools the Natives

Christopher Columbus

I
t was Columbus's fourth and final voyage while exploring the coast of Central America. He found himself in dire straits.

Shipworms ate the planking of his ships. Columbus was forced to abandon two of his ships and to beach the other two caravels in Jamaica.

The natives welcomed the castaways, providing them with food and shelter. As the days dragged into weeks, tensions between the natives and the sailors mounted.

The natives were growing weary of supplying cassava, corn and fish in exchange for tin whistles, trinkets, hawk's bells and other rubbishy goods.

After being stranded for more than six months, the natives stopped supplying Columbus and his crew with food or any other supplies.

When supplies stopped, half of Columbus' crew mutinied. The sailors raided villages for supplies and performed other atrocities, including rape and murder.

. Columbus and his crew were left without a significant source of food or any means to leave the island. With famine now threatening, Columbus formulated a desperate, albeit ingenious plan.

Columbus had certain astronomical tables with him, including the ephemeris compiled by the German astronomer Johannes Muller von Konigsberg, better known by his Latin name, Regiomontanus.

The almanac contained astronomical tables covering the years 1475-1506. Columbus noted the date and timing of an upcoming lunar eclipse.

He requested a meeting with the Cacique, the leader, and told him that his god was angry with the local people's treatment of Columbus and his men.

Columbus told the leader that his god would provide a clear sign of his displeasure by making the rising full Moon appear "inflamed with wrath."

The lunar eclipse and the red moon appeared on schedule. The indigenous people were impressed and frightened.

Columbus' son, Ferdinand, wrote: "With great howling and lamentation they came running from every direction to the ships. They were laden with provisions, praying the Admiral to intercede by all means with God on their behalf; that he not visit his wrath upon them.

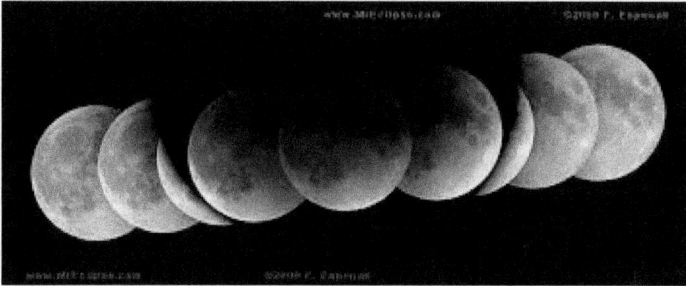

A lunar eclipse allowed Christopher Columbus to fool the natives of Jamaica.

Columbus excused himself to go to his cabin to "pray". He timed the eclipse with his hourglass. Shortly before the eclipse ended after 48 minutes, Columbus told the frightened indigenous people that they were going to be forgiven.

When the moon started to reappear from the shadow of the earth, Columbus told them that his god had pardoned them.

22
Andrew Jackson Kills
Man in a Duel

Andrew Jackson

Andrew Jackson, the man who would one day be President, was hot tempered, physically violent and fond of dueling.

The argument started when Charles Dickinson accused Jackson of cheating on a horse race and of insulting his wife, Rachel.

The horse race was actually between Jackson and Dickinson's father-in-law, Joseph Erwin. Jackson had confronted Dickinson over his slurring remarks about Rachel. Dickinson said if he had made the remarks it was because he was drunk. He apologized.

Jackson and Erwin had scheduled their horse race several months previously. The stakes specified a winning pot of $2,000 to be paid by the loser. There would be a forfeiture of $800 if a horse couldn't run.

Erwin's horse came up lame and he paid the forfeiture amount. It was a dispute over this amount and how it was paid that led up to the duel.

Dickinson accused Jackson of reneging on a horse-racing bet. He called Jackson a coward and an equivocator. He called Rachel, Jackson's wife, a bigamist. (Rachel had married Jackson not knowing her first husband had failed to finalize their divorce).

After the insult to Rachel and a statement published in the National Review, in which Dickinson called Jackson a worthless scoundrel and, again, a coward, Jackson challenged Dickinson to a duel.

Dueling was outlawed in Tennessee. On May 30, 1806, Jackson and Dickinson met at Harrison's Mills on the Red River in Logan, Kentucky. At the first signal from their seconds, Dickinson fired, hitting Jackson in the chest next to his heart.

Dickinson's shot broke two of Jackson's ribs and lodged two inches from his heart.

Jackson put his hand over the wound to staunch the flow of blood, but stayed standing long enough to fire his own weapon.

His gun misfired, and then Jackson aimed and fired again. Doctors determined the bullet in Jackson was too close to his heart to operate. Although Jackson recovered, he suffered chronic pain from the wound for the rest of his life.

Jackson was not prosecuted for murder, and the duel had little effect on his successful campaign for the presidency in 1829. Many men, especially in the South, viewed dueling as a time-honored tradition.

In fact, Rachel's divorce raised more of a scandal in the press and in the parlors than the killing of Dickinson.

In 1804, Thomas Jefferson's vice president Aaron Burr avoided charges after killing former Treasury Secretary and founding father Alexander Hamilton in a duel.

Though accepted by the code of the times, many people considered it cold-blooded killing. The duel cast an aspersion over Jackson's character for the rest of his life and many people in Nashville thought he was "dishonorable" for not concluding the duel once his gun misfired.

Duels of honor, fought primarily between two noblemen, were generally fought over personal insults.

These duels were governed by codes, the most famous of which is the *Code Duello*, a list of 26 rules drafted in 1777 by Irish Duelers. An

American version of the code was drafted in 1838 by South Carolina Governor John Lyde Wilson.

Under the code, a duel was negotiated through companions of the two duelers, known as "seconds". In America, duels were most prevalent in the South, particularly among upper class gentlemen. Men who were challenged to a duel were expected to accept. Those who refused faced public embarrassment.

One South Carolina genntleman, recalling a duel in his youth, remarked, "Well, I never did clearly understand what it was about, but you know it was a time when all gentlemen fought."

Even those who opposed dueling, such as Sam Houston, Henry Clay and Alexander Hamilton, participated in duels due in large part to social pressure.

It was a shift in public opinion, rather than legislation that brought about a decline in dueling. After the Civil War, dueling was no longer popularly accepted in American Society.

It is said that Abraham Lincoln nearly fought in a saber duel in 1842. Lincoln humiliated his fellow state legislator James Shields in a letter to the editor of a newspaper.

Shields challenged him to a duel. Since Lincoln was challenged by Shields, he had the privilege of choosing the weapons to be used. He chose cavalry broadswords "of the largest size".

"I didn't want the damned fellow to kill me, which I think he would have done if we had selected pistols." Lincoln said for his own part, he did not want to kill Shields and "felt sure he could disarm him with a blade."

President Lincoln and James Shields

The two men arrived at Bloody Island, Missouri to face death or victory. As the two men faced each other, with a plank between them that allowed neither to cross, Lincoln swung his sword high above Shields to cut through a nearby tree branch.

This act demonstrated the immensity of Lincoln's reach and strength and was enough to show Shields that he was at a fatal disadvantage.

With the encouragement of bystanders, the two men declared a true. Two decades later, the Civil War brought the two men together again. Shields was now a Brigadier General in the Army of the Potomac and Lincoln was President with ability to promote or demote military officers.

Shields delivered Stonewall Jackson's only defeat at the Battle of Kernstown and was gravely wounded in the process. Lincoln nominated him for a promotion to Major General, symbolically burying all ill-feelings between the men.

During His First Duel, Alexandre Dumas' Pants Fell Down

On a bitter cold day in 1825, famed novelist and playwright Alexander Dumas fought in his first duel.

Duma was having dinner with a group of friends. After eating, the group decided to leave to smoke and play billiards at a local cafe.

A soldier in the café was making fun of Dumas' cloak and boots. Dumas didn't take the slight kindly and a duel was set in a local quarry.

On the day of the duel, it was cold and snowy. Dumas' opponent asked Dumas to take off not only his jacket but also his vest and shirt. While doing this, Dumas also removed his suspenders.

At this point, his pants fell down because his belt buckle was broken. Quarry workers all enjoyed a good laugh.

Dumas tied up his pants with his suspenders and the two opponents went en-garde. Dumas ended up winning the duel after he managed to graze the man with the tip of his ice-cold blade.

This caused his opponent to jump back, tripping on a root. Now on the ground, the man yielded.

23

Gambling

In the

Wild West

A game of Faro is being played in the old West.

Gambling, sharpshooters and cowboys dominated the Wild West. Cowboys loved to gamble, but they weren't usually very good at it. For this reason, card sharps and hustlers kept a ready eye pealed for the gullible cowboy.

The first games of poker, according to R.F. Foster, writing in Foster's Complete Hoyle, was the Persian game of *As Nas*. David Parlett, a gaming historian, challenges Foster's contention. He says poker is a direct derivative of a game called *poque*. This is a French game similar to poker.

As the historians argue, it seems most probable that many of the earlier games influenced the development of poker as it exists today.

When poker was first played in the United States, each player was dealt five cards from a 20-card deck.

Poker's unique features have to do with betting which was not associated with the earlier versions. As the game spread throughout the Mississippi River region in the mid-18th century, it was played in a variety of forms. Sometimes it had 52 cards, and included both straight poker and stud poker.

Twenty card poker is a variant for two players. It is a common English practice to reduce the deck in card games when there are fewer players.

Sometimes, ridiculous assertions are made about the antiquity of poker. By reason alone, it can be said that poker did not exist before *playing cards* themselves were invented.

Playing cards first reached Europe about 1360, but not from China as many attest. They came from the Islamic Mamluk Empire of Egypt through the trading port of Venice.

In the Wild West, poker was king. Gambling was considered a profession as legitimate as the clergy, law or medicine.

The hot game of the Wild West was faro, sometimes called faro bank. Faro is a late 17th century French gambling card game in that it is played between a banker and several players.

Faro was played by the masses due to its fast action, easy-to-learn rules, and better odds than most other games of chance. Faro is played with only one deck of cards and allows for any numbers of players, who are usually referred to as "punters".

Typically, cowboys in the old west would bet on anything that moved, whether it was a foot-race, a boxing match or a flea-jumping contest. There were bull and bear fights, dog fights, cock fights and rodeo events for cowboys.

Horse racing was wildly popular, and it was followed in popularity by boxing. Boxers wore no gloves and a round lasted until one of the fighters was knocked down. As long as the fighters could throw a punch, the match was active.

In modern English, a *casino* is a facility which houses and accommodates gambling activities. The term casino is of Italian origin. The root word is *Casa*, (house) and originally meant a small country villa or summerhouse. The word was changed to refer to a building used for pleasure.

John Law, a Scotsman and professional gambler, was an advisor to the regent Philippe of Orleans. He had a grand plan to populate the

French Louisiana colony and make himself a bundle of money at the same time.

Law's fraudulent scheme called for combining the Bank of France and a land speculation company called the Company of the West.

In 1716, he signed a contract with the government of France, blessed by Philippe, allowing him to establish a private bank which provided him with all the credit he needed.

John Law

Law's plan was to induce noblemen and rich middle class businessmen to buy shares of stock in Louisiana land and to purchase some land for themselves. He also wanted to entice the poor of Europe to become *engagés* (hired hands) for the company.

Using his political clout, Law replaced the governor of Louisiana, Jean Michiele (Governor

1717-1718) with his own man, Bienville (1701-1713).

Paupers, prisoners and prostitutes were sent to populate the colony and start the flow of wealth to the stockholders.

John Law's career ended when the bubble burst in 1720. The French national debt had swollen from 64 to 130 million livres. Now bankrupt, Laws fled Paris in a borrowed coach.

The first gambling casino in America was opened in New Orleans about 1822 by John Davis, an émigré from Saint-Domingue. Davis put up a complex of buildings on Orleans Street, between Bourbon and Royal Streets, which included the Davis Hotel, the Orleans Ballroom, and the Theatre d'Orleans.

The facility was open 24-hours a day and provided gourmet food, liquor, roulette wheels, Faro tables, poker and other games.

Davis, the owner, made sure that "painted ladies" were always at hand for the lusty gamblers.

According to some historians, New Orleans once had a street named Craps. As the story is told, a wealthy Creole named Bernard Marigny (1775-1868) returned to New Orleans from schooling in England. He introduced an intriguing dice game played with two dice.

There was a mutual dislike between Creoles and Americans. The Americans called the Creoles "Johnny Crapaud", a French term for frog. The word was shortened to craps and craps it remains. The street named Craps was renamed Burgundy Street.

Typical of old west gamblers was George Devol.

George Devol didn't like school. He played hooky often and was prone to fighting with his school mates. When his teacher whipped him to correct his attitude and demeanor, he turned on him, hitting him with stones he carried in his pockets for that very purpose.

His father, a ship's carpenter, spent much of his time away. His mother called a neighbor to help her punish the incorrigible George when her husband was away.

At ten years of age, the unmanageable George ran away. He worked as a cabin boy on a river boat steamer called the *Wacousta*. Despite his age, he was efficient at the job, and soon moved to a better-paying job on a boat called the *Walnut Hills*.

George next hired aboard the *Cicero* where he learned to play *Seven-up*. He also learned the art of bluffing. At a mere 15 years of age, George mastered many of the skills of the card sharp, becoming an expert at *Seven-up* and poker.

He loved winning money playing high stakes poker against ministers. After cleaning them out of their cash, he returned their money. "Go and sin no more," he would say.

George didn't exhibit the same qualities when he played against businessmen, soldiers and farmers who frequented the riverboats. He showed no pity with them.

As he got older, George extended his wanderings, traveling throughout the West in search of poker action.

On a train trip, he cleaned out one of the railroad's directors. Thereafter, the director banned all forms of gaming aboard his trains.

George once said, "I don't know just how thick my old skull is, but I do know that it is pretty thick, or it would have been cracked many years ago. I have been struck some terrible blows on my head with iron dray-pins, fireplace pokers, clubs, stone-coal, and boulders. They would have split any man's skull wide open unless it was pretty thick"

George Devol is characterized as the greatest riverboat gambler in the history of the Mississippi River . (Google Images)

As a teenager on the riverboats, George studied his craft well. He watched the professional gamblers with a close eye. He was determined to follow in their footsteps.

By the time George was in his early teens, he could deal seconds, palm cards and recover the cut. He was also depicted as a con artist and a fighter.

George used his forehead as a weapon on numerous occasions. Fighting continued to be a natural part of his life. He soon developed superior skills with a gun.

When the Mexican War broke out Devol thought it a good idea to join the fight and found a job as a barkeeper on the *Corvette*, bound for the Rio Grande and Mexico. While aboard the *Corvette*, he met a card player who taught him how to "stack a deck". Once he reached the Rio Grande, he was proficient enough to put his new-found talent to use.

George Devol

"After cheating all the soldiers I could at cards and there was no one else to rob", George wrote in his autobiography, he returned to New Orleans. "I had about $2,700 and was not quite 17 years old", he recalled. It was the heyday of riverboats.

George returned home to Ohio where he learned to play Faro and Rondo.

Although Devol could operate Keno and Roulette games and considered himself a good poker player, his favorite hustle was Monte. It was simple to play and easy to cheat.

He again worked the riverboats, and soon joined with other card sharps, including Canada Bill Jones, Bill Rollins, and Big Alexander.

Devol left nothing to chance. Decks of cards were commonly provided by the bartender; so Devol supplied bartenders with his custom-made marked decks and paid them well for their complicity.

He saw the opportunities facing him and he began to follow the railroad expansion between Kansas City and Cheyenne in the early 1870s.

Devol was working the Gold Room Saloon in Cheyenne when he witnessed Wild Bill Hickok place a $50 bet, which he lost. He then placed another $50 bet, winning this time, however, the dealer handed him back just $25.

When Bill questioned this, the dealer stated that the house limit was $25. Hickok declared, "You took $50 when I lost," to which the dealer responded "Fifty goes when you lose."

The quick tempered Hickok wasn't about to accept those terms and quickly whacked the dealer on the head with his walking stick, turned over the table, and stuffed his pockets full.

It is estimated that Devol won more than two million dollars in his 40 years of gambling on the riverboats. However, when he died in Hot Springs, Arkansas in 1903, he was almost penniless.

Luke Short was a professional gambler, but he also had a gunman's reputation for having killed 14 men. He was only wounded once.

Luke Short

Short developed a reputation as a violent young man and he admitted to killing several Native Americans in his teens.

He arrived in Abilene in 1870, where he plied his hand at gambling. He was also involved in selling alcohol to the Sioux in Nebraska.

Luke hunted buffalo for their hides during the years 1874-75. He was once arrested for trading whiskey to Indians for buffalo robes. He escaped the army escort taking him to Omaha for trial on this charge.

His biography notes that he made his way to Denver, and never again worked except as a high rolling professional gambler.

Luke was the son of a sharecropper, born in 1854. He always remained thin as a rail. His stature attracted the notice of Judge Stordon, a horseman from Nashville. Stordon took Luke under his wing and taught him jockeying.

When Stordon thought his young protégé was ready, they headed for Hot Springs, Arkansas. Short won several races, endearing him to the ladies. He became so adept at blackjack and poker that he won the purses of riders and grooms in jockey rooms. Stordon was impressed with Short's gambling prowess.

The two then posed as indolent transients. They pooled their money and visited all the gambling parlors in St. Louis, New Orleans and San Francisco.

When Stordon died of a heart attack, Short struck out on his own, carrying a leather gripsack filled with double eagles and a hidden pistol to protect himself and his investment.

He started wearing fancy attire, and among the miners he fleeced, he became known as "the gentleman gambler."

Eventually, bad luck overtook him, and he ended up broke. He then returned to the cow towns, working as a bartender and part-time house gambler.

For ten years, Dodge City, Kansas was said to thrive on whiskey. City politics revolved around whiskey and Dodge became known as the "Wickedest Little City in America".

Colonel Richard I. Dodge assumed command of Fort Dodge in 1872 and stopped the sale of alcohol at the fort. This edict affected not only the soldiers, but also the buffalo hunters and traders in western Kansas.

At the same time, the Atchison, Topeka & Santa Fe Railroad was laying track toward Fort Dodge, bringing hundreds of workers, most of whom wanted whiskey.

George Kennedy, a twenty-four-year-old Canadian, seized on what he thought was a masterful profit-making idea. He brought a wagonload of whiskey back from eastern Kansas to Fort Dodge. He set up five miles outside of Fort Dodge and opened for business, charging twenty-five cents a drink. He became a wealthy man.

Luke Short bought the Long Branch Saloon in Dodge City. He soon became the target of an organized group called the Commercial Detective Agency. This was, in reality, a front for extorting money from saloons and gambling casinos. The chief collector was "Longhaired" Jim Courtright, considered one of the fastest draws in Texas.

His cross draw gave him the reputation of being equal to, if not superior, to the likes of Wild Bill Hickok, Johnny Ringo, and Wes Hardin. Most saloon owners generally paid up rather than go against Courtright.

One evening, Courtright strolled into Luke Short's saloon to collect the extortion money.

"Go to Hell!" Luke told him

"I'll be back," Courtright snarled, "and you'd better pay up!"

While Short's friends urged him to comply with Courtright's demands, Luke remained adamant.

When Courtright returned the next evening, Short was running the roulette wheel. Courtright asked him for the money.

"I have no intention of paying, is that plain enough," Short told him.

Longhaired Jim went for his gun, but Short beat him to the draw. He fired a split second before Courtright, severing the extortionist's thumb on his gun hand. When Courtright attempted to toss his gun to his other hand, Luke fired again. The bullet caught Courtright squarely between the eyes.

W.H. Harris, a candidate for mayor, was a partner in Luke's saloon. The opposition candidate for mayor backed Luke's saloon competition.

When the election was held, Harris lost and the new mayor passed ordinances to suppress brothels and vagrants. Two days later, three women employed as singers in Luke's Long Branch Saloon were arrested. No similar arrests were made at competing saloons, however.

Saloonkeepers, including Luke Short, who were not favored by the new mayor were arrested under the city's new anti-gambling laws and told to get on the next train that was leaving town. Some 150 citizens were put on watch to make sure they did not come back.

Luke settled in Kansas City, and was kept informed of the situation in Dodge City, where the tension continued to escalate. Bat Masterson came to Kansas City to help his friend Luke Short.

Masterson was ex-sheriff of Ford County and had previously crossed with the same men now faced by Luke Short. A short time later, more of Luke's friends arrived, including Wyatt Earp, Joe

Lowe, known as "Rowdy Joe", Shotgun Collins, and Doc Holliday.

The news that these famous gunslingers were joining Luke Short in his fight against Dodge City's mayor did cause a furor. The matter was eventually settled when the city allowed Short to pay a one-thousand-dollar-fine and reopen his business.

Gambling was again legalized and ornate screen doors were put on the front of the establishments to bar the view of passersby.

Luke sold the Long Branch in 1884. With the money from the sale, he opened up the White Elephant saloon in Fort Worth, Texas. The establishment had a luxurious billiard room. The money rolled in.

During his early days, Luke was referred to as a "white Indian". He is said to have been an Indian in every respect except color. He was a little fellow, only about five feet, six inches in height, and weighing perhaps one hundred forty pounds soaking wet.

His head was somewhat larger than the rest of his body. It required a seven-and-one-eighth-inch hat to fit his well-shaped round head.

Luke Short had received none of the advantages in school. He could barely write his name legibly. After Luke left home at thirteen years of age for cutting up a school bully, he worked as a thirty-dollar-a-month cowboy, driving cattle from Texas to the Kansas rail towns.

Frank Dowler, an old-time sheriff of Palmdale, California, knew well Luke Short's history.

"Seldom did anyone make a laughing remark about his height, or the fact the name Short might refer to his shortness."

Short was sometimes referred to as "Dapper Luke". He wore a silk, stovepipe hat, a fancy braided shirt with ruffles, and a diamond stickpin in his tie.

Some referred to Luke Short as the "Undertaker's Friend," because he "shot 'em where it didn't show."

In August 1893, Luke, his wife, and his brother, Young, went to Geuda Springs, Kansas in Sumner County to bathe in the health-restoring waters. Luke had dropsy. In less than a month, he died. His remains were buried in Oakwood Cemetery in Fort Worth.

Doc Holliday, said lawman Wyatt Earp, "...was the most skillful gambler, and the nerviest, fastest, deadliest man with a six-gun I ever saw."

This indeed is great praise for a man who studied dentistry and occasionally practiced his craft. He is said to have been a good dentist, but learned soon after starting his practice that he had tuberculosis.

He contacted a number of doctors, but most agreed he had only a few months to live. He was told to seek a drier climate. In 1873, Holliday packed his bags, boarded a train, and got off in Dallas, Texas, the end of the railroad line.

Doc Holliday

Holiday hung again out his dentist shingle, but the coughing spells caused by his tuberculosis forced him to curtail his practice.

He sometimes broke out coughing during the most embarrassing moments, such as in the middle of filling a tooth or during the extraction of one.

Holliday had a talent for gambling. This quickly became his sole means of support. Because of the hazards involved with being a professional gambler, he practiced long and hard in shooting and knife skills.

The only thing faster than Holiday's draw was his temper.

After a provocation, in which Holliday put two shots into a Dallas citizen, he was forced to flee Dallas, steps ahead of a posse. He stopped at the tough little cow town of Jacksboro, in Jacks County, where he took a job dealing Faro.

Holliday carried a gun in a shoulder holster, another one on his hip, and a long wicked knife. In a short span of time, he became involved in three gunfights. In one, he left a man dead. No legal action was taken against him.

He became so careless that he killed a soldier from Fort Richardson. The U.S. Government jumped into this investigation, and Holliday, knowing he would be stretched by a rope if caught, fled. He headed for Apache country in Colorado.

The hot-tempered Holliday could not stop getting involved in arguments. He killed three more men before he reached Denver.

Doc traveled west knowing he had a short time to live. Actually, the drier climate added an extra fifteen years to his tortuous, tubercular existence.

Doc Holliday ended up in Fort Griffin, Texas. There he met the only woman ever to come into his life. She was called "Big Nose" Kate. She was a dance-hall girl and prostitute and had a temper that matched that of Holliday.

It was in John Shanssey's saloon where Holliday met both Big Nose Kate and lawman Wyatt Earp. Earp rode into town in search of train robber Dave Rudabaugh. Doc helped Earp gain some of the information he needed for Rudabaugh's arrest and they became friends.

Doc could not avoid trouble and he never ran away from it. One day, a would-be tough guy named Ed Bailey sat down in a poker game with Holliday. To irritate Doc, Bailey kept picking up the discards and looking through them.

Big Nose Kate

"Don't do that," Holliday warned, noting it was against the rules of western poker and anyone scanning the discards would forfeit the pot. When Bailey did it again, Doc reached across the table, and, without showing his hand, raked in the pot.

Bailey brought a six-shooter from under the table while Doc brought out a large knife. Before Bailey could pull the trigger, Doc had slashed his belly open. Thinking he was right in defending himself against the card cheater, Doc allowed the marshal to arrest him.

He miscalculated because when Holliday was disarmed and locked up, Bailey's friends clamored for Holliday's blood. Big Nose Kate knew she had to do something quick or Doc was finished.

She swung into action by setting fire to an old shed. It burned rapidly and threatened to engulf the town. The only three people that didn't rush to fight the fire were Doc, his guard, and Kate. When Kate saw the guard and the prisoner alone, she stepped in with a pistol in each hand. She disarmed the guard, handed another pistol to Doc and they flew away in the night.

When they arrived in Dodge City, they registered at Deacon Cox's boarding house as Dr. and Mrs. J.H. Holliday. Kate gave up prostitution and quit inhabiting saloons. Doc hung out his shingle again.

Finally, Kate told Doc she could no longer stand this dull existence and went back to the saloons and a life of prostitution. Doc went back to dealing Faro in the Long Branch saloon.

Doc was known to consume as much as four quarts of whiskey in a day. Sometimes, he drank a pint before breakfast. This was the only medicine that relieved his tubercular cough. Still, he never appeared drunk.

When a number of Texas cowboys came into town with a herd of cattle, word arrived at the Long Branch that several of the trail drivers had cornered Wyatt Earp and intended to shoot him down.

Gun in hand, Doc leaped through the barroom door. He found two cowboys holding cocked revolvers on Wyatt, goading him to draw before they shot him down. Other cowboys stood by, taunting and insulting Earp.

"Pray and jerk your gun," roared Morrison, one of the cowboys, "your time has come, Earp."

Another voice rang out behind Morrison.

"No, friend, you draw or throw your hands up," said Doc Holliday, with his pistol at Morrison's temple. "Any of you bastards pulls a gun and your leader here loses what's left of his brains." The armed cowboys dropped their guns.

Shouting a stream of profanities, Doc distracted the cowboys long enough for Wyatt to rap the leader over the head with a pistol, then set about relieving the other cowboys of their guns.

Wyatt never forgot the fact that Doc Holliday saved his life that night.

After another fight with Kate, Doc drifted out of town, locating in Trinidad, Colorado. There, a young gambler known as "Kid Colton" badgered Doc into a fight. Doc's hot temper flared. He fired twice and Colton lay dead in the street.

Doc headed out of town again, landing in Las Vegas, New Mexico. He opened a dental office again, but the new try at being respectable didn't work.

He got into an argument with Mike Gordon, a popular man among the locals. Not hesitating, Doc invited him to start shooting when he was ready. Gordon was killed by three shots into the stomach.

Doc had to get out of town in a hurry. He decided to go back to Dodge City, where he would be safe, since Wyatt Earp there was his friend.

When he arrived in Dodge City, Earp had taken a lawman's job in Tombstone, Arizona, where he intended to meet with his brothers, James, Virgil and Morgan. Holiday decided to join Earp in Tombstone.

There was a nest of outlaws in Tombstone that deemed the town as their private domain. They didn't like the arrival of the Earp brothers, nor of Doc Holliday.

Included among these outlaws, known locally as the "Cowboys", were Ike and Billy Clanton, Frank and Tom McLaury, and Johnny Ringo. The "Cowboys" threatened to kill the Earps and Doc Holliday if they didn't get out of town.

As everyone in Tombstone knew, neither the Earps nor Holliday would run. Virgil received word the Cowboys were gathering at the O.K. Corral and that they were armed, which was against City law.

Doc met Wyatt, Morgan and Virgil Earp on Fourth Street on their way to the O.K. Corral. Doc insisted on going with them where five armed men, all potential killers, waited in a vacant lot behind the OK Corral, between Flys Photo Studio and the Harwood house.

The fight was short-lived. Wyatt Earp and Billy Clanton started the battle. Wyatt shot Billy in the chest. He then cut Tom McLaury down with a double charge of buckshot.

A bullet from Frank McLaury cut into Doc's pistol holster and burned a nasty crease across his hip. Doc's return fire smashed into McLaury's brain.

The fight lasted less than 30 seconds. Virgil Earp had been shot in the leg, Morgan through both shoulders. Only Wyatt had emerged from the fight unscathed.

Doc Holliday's health was failing fast. He went to Glenwood Springs, Colorado to try the sulfur baths. His health was too far-gone. He spent his last fifty-seven days in bed, delirious fourteen of those days.

One morning, he awoke clear-eyed and asked for a glass of whiskey. He drank it down quickly, and, looking at his bare toes sticking out at the end of the bed, said, "This is funny". He died without his boots on at 35 years of age.

Poker Alice

Poker Alice was just about as famous for her gambling abilities as were many of the male gamblers. Her name was Alice Ivers Duffield.

While a devout gambler, she was just as adamant about observing the Sabbath. She was willing to shoot anyone violating this sacred observance.

Poker Alice was a cigar-smoking woman who could hold her own with any man at the gambling table or at the bar. She was wise enough never to touch alcohol while gambling, however.

Alice was born in England and came to America as a teenager.

At the age of twenty, Alice married Frank Duffield who worked in the Leadville, Colorado mines. Frank was an enthusiastic poker player when not working, and he frequented several of the gambling halls in Leadville.

Alice went with Frank to avoid being home alone. Standing behind her husband and watching the play, Alice was a quick study and soon joined in the games, demonstrating her proficiency at both poker and faro.

Frank Duffield worked at a dangerous trade in the silver mines of Leadville. He was killed while resetting an unexploded dynamite charge.

Alice was left with no means of support. She was well-educated, however, and might have been a good school teacher. There was a shortcoming to this possibility. Leadville boasted a population of 35,000, but had no school.

She developed into one of the most fearsome gamblers in the west. Her talent lay in a truly astounding dexterity. She could manipulate cards as well as any magician.

Alice perfected her technique and moved further west. She became such a tactical gambler that she broke the bank at one casino. This allowed her to go on a New York City spending spree.

Alice was in high demand, both as a player and as a dealer. She was described as a five-foot-four, comely blue eyed woman wearing stylish clothing.

Alice traveled from one mining camp to another, testing her poker luck and stamina at each stop. She was a rare thing indeed. She was a *lady* in a gambling hall, but was not one of the so-called "Ladies of the Evening."

She picked up the habit of smoking cigars as she plied her card profession. To let her opponents know she was their equal, Alice carried a .38 revolver and wasn't afraid to use it. Being a woman, Alice attracted attention and men were honored to play poker with her. Gambling halls welcomed her, figuring she was "good for business".

At one time, she worked in Bob Ford's saloon in Creede, Colorado—the same Bob Ford that shot Jesse James.

Her travels soon took her to Deadwood, South Dakota. There she became friendly with Warren G. Tubbs, a housepainter with a gambling habit.

Alice routinely beat him at the gambling tables and Tubbs became infatuated with her. When a drunken miner threatened Warren Tubbs with a knife, Alice pulled out her .38 and shot the drunk in the arm.

Tubbs and Alice married and bought a ranch near Sturgis, South Dakota on the Moreau River. Alice was forced to reduce her time gambling for she and Tubbs had seven children.

Tuberculosis claimed Tubbs in 1910. One account says Alice loaded his body in a horse-drawn wagon to take him to Sturgis for burial. Another legend maintains that she had pawned her wedding ring to pay for the funeral.

The same account says that after the funeral she went to a gambling hall and won the money back so she could reclaim her wedding ring.

Alice had to earn a living and she had a ranch to tend.. She hired George Huckert to work her homestead and she moved to Sturgis. Huckert became enamored by her and pleaded with her to marry him.

She finally agreed saying flippantly, "I owed him so much in back wages, I figured it would be cheaper to marry him than pay him off. The marriage was short-lived, as Huckert died in 1913.

Alice opened a saloon between Sturgis and Fort Meade called "Poker's Palace". Her establishment featured poker games, liquor and women to service customers.

A drunken soldier once caused a ruckus in the saloon, breaking furniture and wreaking havoc. Alice handled the matter. She drew her .38 and shot the man.

She was arrested and jailed. In jail, she whiled away her time smoking cigars and reading the Bible. Alice was acquitted of the charge but authorities closed her saloon.

In her later years, with her fancy gowns gone, Alice struggled. She was in her 70s, and continued to gamble. She started wearing men's clothing. "At my age, I suppose I should be knitting. But I would rather play poker with five or six experts than eat."

Crede, Colorado

In her later years, she opened a house of ill-repute. She was arrested often for keeping a disorderly house and for drunkenness. She paid her fines but continued to operate the business.

She was next arrested for her repeated convictions of running a brothel. She was sent to prison. At age 75, she was pardoned by the governor.

Alice died from complications of gall-bladder surgery at age 79. She claimed to have won more than $250,000 at the gaming tables and never once cheated.

One of her favorite sayings was, *"Praise the Lord and place your bets. I'll take your money with no regrets."*

Benjamin Marks

At 13, Benjamin Marks served as a dispatch bearer in the Civil War. At nineteen, he dealt three-card Monte on a board suspended from his shoulders.

Marks called himself a gambler, but in fact he was a confidence man. The object was to steer his victim into a trap, leading him to think he was in on the inside of a good thing, and then milk him dry.

Ben found the uproarious days of the "Hell on Wheels" were gone. Competition in the gambling tents was too tough.

The completion of the transcontinental railroad west from Omaha and the railroad lines from Chicago into Council Bluffs proved a situation ripe for the plucking to a certain class of criminal.

These were the confidence men and the wily skills shown on the muddy streets of Council Bluffs and Omaha during the late 19th century. The growth of the railroads provided an ease of access, plenty of strangers, and a centralized location from which to operate.

Marks hit upon an idea to "revolutionize the grift". The grift is a swindle, hustle, or scam that uses the victim's own greed to lure money or valuables away from him. There is a widely known maxim in the world of the grift, "You can't cheat and honest man."

Ben Mark's new system included setting up a storefront. In Cheyenne, Ben posted a sign on a building reading, "The Dollar Store".

In the store window, he exhibited all kinds of merchandise, each item obviously worth more than one dollar. Inside, Marks and his cohorts would wait. Bargain hunters and people looking for something for nothing began to appear.

Once the potential suckers were inside, their interest was shifted from the so-called dollar bargains to a three-card Monte game being dealt on a wooden barrel.

Since no customer ever left the Monte game with any money in his pocket, none of the merchandise was ever sold.

The game really caught on and scores of Monte stores were scattered in cities throughout the West. Accomplices called Steerers and Ropers frequented hotels, rail and stage terminals to find suckers and bring them to the dollar stores.

The next step in the development of The Big Store was its transition from a simple lure to a stage for a particular form of fraud. This change was accompanied by an increase in the sophistication of the cons which made use of the store.

To use an example: In the fight-store con, a roper would pose as the employee of a wealthy man, and claim that this man was the sponsor of a boxer, with whom he travelled about the country, taking on local competition.

The roper would explain that the boxer disliked his employer, and intended to defraud him: The roper and the boxer had agreed that the boxer would intentionally lose the next fight, and that the roper would arrange to bet against him. Naturally, the roper could not do this in the open, and needed an accomplice (the mark) to bet on his behalf.

In the fight-store con, the store was set up with a boxing ring, and a large number of "spectators", all of whom were betting with vigor. The effect of this was to convince the "mark" of the truth of the roper's story, and to persuade him that it would be a good idea to bet some of his own money (along with that given to him by the roper) in order to make a quick profit.

Naturally, this would all end in tears for the mark, as the wealthy man's boxer would "accidentally" "kill" his opponent, sending everyone running for the exits.

An ironic twist to the Dollar Store scam was that a dollar store operator in Chicago found they could make more money selling items for one dollar than they could running the scams. The owner founded a national chain of legitimate department stores, selling goods for one dollar.

Ben Marks also ran another enterprise. He and his wife Mary had a big three-story log farmhouse in Elk Grove just outside of Council Bluffs, Iowa. It was called the "Hog Ranch". The house straddled the county line.

Ben's wife, Mary, was a successful madam and a larger than life character in her own right. When law officers from one county would raid her place, Mary sent the girls to the other end of the room— across county lines and out of the policemen's jurisdiction.

Marks is said to be one of the success stories in the con game business who didn't throw everything away through high living and gambling.

He died of liver failure in 1918. He was seventy-one years of age.

Kitty Leroy was pretty, a gunfighter, a performer and some said a prostitute. Her most famous trait, however, was that she was one of the most proficient poker players in the west.

Kitty began dancing publicly at the age of ten. As she got older, she began working in dance halls and saloons.

She became proficient in the handling of firearms, and more important, she became a skilled card player.

Kitty married her first husband at age 15. The marriage was doomed to failure because of Kitty's promiscuousness. She ventured west. By 20 years of age, she married a second time.

She became one of the most popular dancing attractions in Dallas, Texas. She gave up dancing to become a faro dealer. Kitty became a skilled dealer and a sharp gambler.

Kitty Leroy

She and her second husband headed for California where they hoped to open a saloon. Kitty soon left her second husband for another man, whom she married. This marriage was short-lived.

According to one report, Kitty and her third husband became embroiled in a serious argument during which she attacked him.

When her husband refused to hit her because she was a woman, Kitty changed into men's clothing and challenged him again. He still refused to hit her because she was a woman.

She drew her gun. He refused to draw his. She shot him. He died a few days later.

Leroy then headed for Deadwood, South Dakota. She traveled in the same wagon train as Calamity Jane and Wild Bill Hickok.

In Deadwood, Kitty worked as a prostitute for a madam named Mollie Johnson.

She then opened the Mint Gambling Saloon and married her fourth husband, this time to a German gold prospector. When his money ran out, they began to argue often. She hit him over the head with a bottle one night and threw him out.

Her saloon was successful. In addition to her saloon income, Leroy occasionally worked as a prostitute, but mostly managed her own girls.

She then married Leroy R. Curley, her fifth and final husband. This too proved to be a volatile marriage as Curley was extremely jealous. Leroy did not help the marriage as she continued having numerous affairs, one of which was with an ex-husband.

According to the Black Hills Daily Times, Sam Curley shot and killed his wife Kitty in the Lone Star Saloon. He then turned the gun on himself.

According to the Black Hills Daily Times her estate was valued at $650.

24

Enter the Velocipede

An engraving titled "The American Velocipede illustrated the ultimate in bicycles.

In the early 1870s, bicycles were fast, exciting and dangerous things that could make an ordinary human feel he was flying with the wind.

Fred T. Merrill worshipped champion trick rider Carrie Moor, a champion bicycle trick rider.

Fred T. Merrill found a ready market for bicycles in Portland. He set up a tent in 1885 and moved into more solid quarters soon after. When public demand shifted to automobiles, so did Merrill's business.

Fred's father opened a riding rink in Lynn, Massachusetts and stocked it with a few two-wheeled velocipedes. These two-wheeled machines were the state of the art in bicycles.

A velocipede was a crude thing, just a step removed from the notorious all-wood "boneshakers" of the 1850s. The velocipede featured a smaller wheel in the back and a larger one in the front. For power, the rider pedaled the machine.

Carrie Moor could make the velocipede dance like a ballerina. Fred found her fascinating.

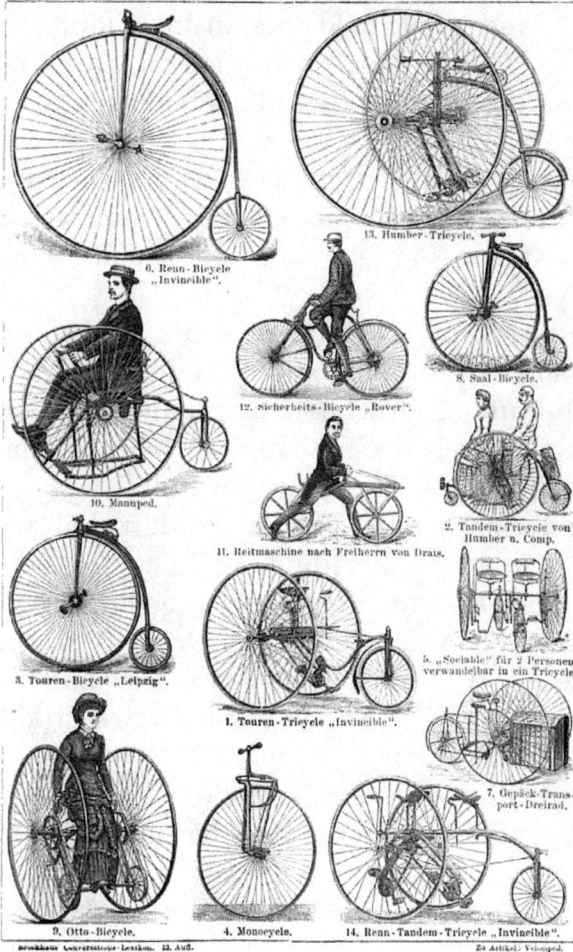

VELOCIPEDE.

This drawing shows various designs of velocipedes.

Young Fred Merrill told the Portland Morning Oregonian newspaper, "Long before we left for the Pacific coast, I was an expert rider, doing all the tricks Carrie Moor knew and inventing some of my own."

The Merrill family moved to San Francisco, where Fred continued his stunt riding. To his surprise, Carrie Moor was also in San Francisco and was the headline act at the Occidental Skating Academy.

Fred apprenticed himself as an engraver. He soon found he could make more money from his bicycle trick riding than he could engraving etchings.

One evening, he built a plank bridge, one foot wide, across the arena and pedaled his brand-new British-built high-wheel "penny-farthing" bicycle across the bridge while his two baby brothers sat on his shoulders. The crowd loved it.

Fred soon heard of an Australian chap who was making waves in Portland as a bicycle trick rider. Fred traveled to Portland and challenged the Aussie to a bicycle-riding contest.

The Australian rider accepted the challenge, but left town that very evening in the dark of night. He was not seen again.

Merrill liked Portland and decided to stay there. In 1885, now convinced that bicycles were here to stay, he opened what was called the first bicycle dealership.

Fred knew that when the new "safety bicycle" was built that he needed to upgrade his dealership. The safety bicycle had two equal size wheels. The rear wheel was driven by a chain and was easy to learn how to use.

This bicycle was going to explode the industry and Fred Merrill intended to be ready when it happened. He talked to the telephone company and bought space on the company's telephone poles to hang a sign with the words "Ride A Rambler". Rambler was his top-selling brand and the sign was in bright red and was seen on telephone poles all over town.

BICYCLES
TYPEWRITERS,
CANOES, ETC.

CASH OR INSTALLMENTS. BOUGHT, SOLD, OR EXCHANGED. 400 WHEELS IN STOCK ALL GRADES AND PRICES, AND ALL WARRANTED. SEND FOR CATALOG AND CLUB DISCOUNTS.
Live Agents Wanted everywhere.

FRED. T. MERRILL,
127 WASHINGTON ST., PORTLAND, OR.

This bicycle ad ran in a 1891 Portland, Oregon newspaper.

He began staging events, including daredevil stunt-riding exhibitions, races against horses. He even had a trick dog, called the "Rambler Dog" that jumped off the roof of his building into a net.

Bicycle liberated the women in Portland, giving them a means of getting around without depending on their brothers or husbands to hitch up a team of horses.

Pastors preached strong sermons against any and all women who took to the deviltry of riding a wheel. There were letters to the paper and editorials about the great menace to life, health and morals of the bicycle.

Bicyclists who rode with excessive speed and carelessness were arrested and taken to jail just as reckless drivers are today.

An unfortunate thing happened to Fred Merrill the bicycle dealer and promoter.

After a solid ten years of wild popularity, a time during which Fred sold more than 50,000 bicycles, the fad went out like a light. The demand for wheels dropped month by month.

The bicycle fad was killed, not by the automobile, but by a group of enterprising prostitutes in the north end of Portland. North End Madam "Liverpool Liz" may have instigated the downward trend for bike sales in Portland.

"Liverpool Liz" invested in a bicycle riding track and equipped her girls with brightly colored outfits. They wore skirts with slits high enough to show as much leg as possible.

They staged races around the track for the gentlemen to bet on. When business was slow, they sallied forth around town on their wheels to troll for customers, ringing their bells and flashing their winning smiles.

Next came Blanche Hamilton's girls adopting the bicycle craze and joining Liverpool Liz's girls.

The society girls got off their wheels and began traveling by foot or returned to the practice of driving a buggy.

It was years before bicycle riding in Portland came back into favor.

25

The Missing Pilot
And the UFO

Felix Moncla, Jr. boards aircraft.

irst Lieutenant Felix Moncla may have
died Nov. 23, 1953. Or, he may not have.
He and his fellow crew member, Lt.
Robert L. Wilson, were chasing a UFO and they
both disappeared at the same time. Both Monclas's
plane and the UFO were seen as two blips on

ground control's radar before they mysteriously disappeared over Lake Superior.

An F-89 Scorpion such as Lt. Felix Moncla was flying.

Air Defense operators were watching their screens when the blip of an unknown machine appeared. In less than two minutes an F-89 from Kimross Field was streaking over the locks in pursuit of the UFO.

Back at GCI (Ground Control Intercept) the controller watched the jet's blip on his radarscope. As it moved toward the UFO's blip, the strange craft changed course.

The controller called Moncla and gave him the new bearing. From the scope he saw that the F-89 was now over Sault Sainte Marie. The UFO, flying fast as a jetliner, was heading toward Lake Superior.

At more than 500 miles an hour, Moncla's F-89 raced after it, out across Whitefish Bay.

Nine more minutes ticked by and the F-89 was closing the gap with the UFO. The controller figured that Wilson, Moncla's radar technician, should have spotted their quarry on the fighter's short-range radar screen.

As the controller watched, the two blips merged into one. One thing seemed grimly certain to the controller. The two machines were locked together, as if in a smashing collision.

A search and rescue operation was quickly mounted, but failed to find a trace of either the plane or the pilot.

Air force investigators reported that Moncla may have experienced vertigo and crashed into the lake. The Air Force said Moncla was known to experience vertigo from time to time.

The official accident report states that when the unknown was first picked up on radar, it was believed to be RCAF aircraft "VC-912", which was classified as UNKNOWN because it was 30 miles off its flight plan course.

When the unidentified craft was finally on radar it was noted that the two radar images, the UFO and the Air Force Jet, were very close and at some point, they intersected but only one remained.

On multiple occasions, the RCAF has denied its involvement in the intercept.

The Air Force has been less than forthcoming about the incident. "We still know nothing about it," said Leoni M. Shannon, Moncla's older sister.

She said government officials were not helpful in providing the family with straight answers.

26

Voyage Led to Cannibalism

A Japanese junk

Little did the 14 sailors realize they were embarking on an epic voyage where only three would survive and from which none would ever return home.

The year was 1832 when the 150-ton Japanese junk, Hojunmaru, capable of carrying 1,200 sacks of rice, set sail and headed towards Edo, now Japan.

It was less than a day into the seemingly routine trip when the skies turned black and violent winds began churning the sea.

The boat was little more than a toy in the roiling waters. Cold seawater began to breach the decks of the Hojunmaru. Then, to make matters worse, a powerful, but unseasonable typhoon struck the boat, leaving it rudderless.

For fear of capsizing, the crew took an axe and chopped down the mast to stabilize the freighter. The strategy worked and the ship rode out the storm.

Now the crew, although thankful to be alive, realized they had an even greater problem. They were aboard a ship without either a rudder shaft or a mast.

Their cargo was a small amount of rice, some Japanese Sake, one barrel of drinking water, and some fine Japanese porcelain for the Shogun in Edo.

The crew drifted helplessly for weeks, and then months. The shifting currents floated them eastward away from Japan.

Realizing their plight, the men did what they could just to stay alive. They made drinking water by boiling seawater with fires fueled by wood pirated from their vessel. They cooked the rice with the Sake.

The lack of proper nourishment began to take its toll. Some crewmen became delirious, others depressed. All contemplated how their fate would be determined. Exposure? Starvation? Madness? Then one by one the sailors began to die.

Overwhelmed by the stench of rotting flesh, the dwindling crew was forced to throw their dead comrades overboard.

As he lowered his older brother into the sea, 14-year-old Otokichi wondered what he had done to deserve this forbidding fate.

The crew was now down to three. After 13 months adrift in the Pacific, they drew near to shore. They had a strange feeling that someone was watching them.

They soon saw the source of their concern. Standing on the shores of Cape Alava in Oregon Territory were dozens of fierce-looking coastal Makah Native Americans.

Their appearance was indeed menacing as they were wearing whalebone jewelry and were wrapped in soft yellow cedar tree bark to keep them warm.

The three crew members felt little joy as they dared to set foot on land. They surrendered to the Makah and begged for mercy. The Makah plundered the ship and enslaved the teenaged crew members, Kyukichi, Otokichi and the slightly older Iwakichi.

Word of the capturing of the crew members was communicated by an Indian scout to "Big Chief", Dr. John McLoughlin, head of the Hudson Bay Company. McLoughlin was headquartered in Fort Vancouver on the Columbia River.

McLoughlin sent out a rescue party of 20 men, but they could not cross the snowcapped peaks of the coastal mountains. They had to return to Vancouver.

When summer arrived, Dr. McLoughlin ordered a ship preparing to sail from Fort Vancouver to stop at Cape Alava and to learn more about the three captives.

If possible, the captain was instructed to buy the men's freedom. Captain O'Neill invited the Makah chief aboard the brig Llama to trade. Once aboard, he took the chief captive in exchange for the three sailors.

Only two of the Chinese sailors were still in the hands of the Makah as Otokichi had gone into the forest with a Makah maiden to collect berries. He was nowhere to be found and the ship left without him.

On the ship's return voyage, Otokichi's freedom was purchased with several cotton blankets that the Makah cherished. The freed sailors were taken to Fort Vancouver in the summer of 1834.

The Japanese crewmen found it difficult to acclimate to their strange new world. They did eventually adjust. They learned English under a missionary sent by the American Board to Oregon Territory.

The young Japanese men wondered if they would ever return home to see their families in Japan again. Then the Brig Eagle arrived at Fort George. The three boys were put aboard.

The Eagle was headed for England, from which the boys were to make their way to Japan on another ship.

On arrival in England, however, Lord Palmerston, the foreign ministry secretary (and future prime minister) would not allow the three Japanese to disembark. They were forced to spend an entire week aboard the Eagle, watching the busy city streets from the rail.

At issue was a disagreement with the Hudson Bay Company over whether the government had a responsibility for the boys' welfare.

The British Government wanted to send the three to their home directly. Dr. McLoughlin saw a bigger opportunity. He intended to send the boys home, but he also saw the possibility of using them to open up trade with Japan.

In the end, the Crown conceded the importance of Japan to expanding Pacific trade. The day before their departure, Lord Palmerston allowed the three sailors one day on shore to see the city.

At last, a half-year later, the trio arrived back in the Far East. They were aboard the HBC ship General Palmer, which dropped anchor off of Macao in December 1835.

The three men realized they were closer to home than they had been in years, but they also realized getting there would not come soon.

Given the importance of the Japanese boys in opening Japanese trade, the three were put in the custody of Charles Elliott, British Consul & Trade Commissioner. The boys were assigned the task of teaching the British the Japanese language under the German missionary, Dr. Karl Friedrich August Gutzlaff.

Finally, they arrived in Napacan, present-day Okinawa, on the ship, The Morrison,. The Morrison was allowed to dock only long enough to load supplies.

While in Port, it was learned that several locals on Okinawa were infected with small pox.

Finally, the Morrison set sail for Edo (Japan). When the first sighting of Japan was made, Iwakichi, a seasoned helmsman, recognized the mouth of Edo Bay.

To the surprise of the ship's officers, they were greeted with cannon fire. This is known historically as "The Morrison Incident".

"How could it be?" the crewmen asked. Five years of involuntary exile, only wishing to return home, and their own country was firing cannons at them.

The actions of the garrison on land should not have come as a surprise. Japan had been closed to outsiders for nearly 200 years. The Shogunate government wasn't about to make an exception for the Morrison.

A cannonball finally struck the hull of the Morrison. The ship retreated to consider their options, including the sending of the Japanese passengers ashore in a small boat or else, trying to land at night.

Rather than risk further damage to the ship, the Morrison sailed south along the Coast of Honshu Island, just out of reach of the cannons.

Soon, Iwakichi began yelling at the top of his lungs. "Tobaura! Tobaura!" He had spotted the small port from where they had originally embarked on their epic adventure in 1832.

He begged the captain to give him a dinghy, but the ship was too far out to reach shore by paddle and Captain Ingersol didn't want to risk sending their already damaged ship closer to land. They continued south, to the disappointment of Otokichi and his friends.

In disbelief, Otokichi turned to the missionary Reverend Williams. He denounced his home country that turned its back on him. He and his other friends knew they could never return.

With that done, Otokichi became a sailor on the Morrison. With no home to return to, he sailed with the Morrison to New York City. He took up residence there briefly at a boarding house for sailors in the East River district of Manhattan.

While sailing later, Otokichi found his old guardian Reverend Williams working at Mission Press in Macao. There, Otokichi was christened and given the name "John" from his work with Mr. Gutzlaff to translate the "Bible of John".

His middle name was Matthew. His last name, Ottosan, had a more curious origin.

When Otokichi first arrived in the Oregon Territory, it was noted that his friend called him "Oto". But to give him proper respect under the Japanese tradition, they added "san" after his name.

27

The Oldest City
In the U.S.

A look at Acoma Pueblo today

Acoma Pueblo has been occupied for more than 800 years, making it the oldest continuously occupied area in the United States. Three villages make up Acoma Pueblo and totals about five million acres of land.

The word "Acoma" is from the Spanish word *Acoma*, which means "the place that always was". Another translation means "People of the White Rock". Pueblo simply means town or village.

Acoma Pueblo is known as "Sky City". It was strategically built atop a 357-foot sandstone mesa for defensive purposes. It was built between 1100 and 1250 A.D.

Acoma Pueblo is located about 60 miles west of Albuquerque, New Mexico. Pueblo people are believed to have descended from the Anasazi, Mogollon and other ancient people.

The site was chosen, in part, because it provided a defensive position for the tribe against raiders. Access to the pueblo was difficult as the faces of the mesa are sheer. It could only be reached by a hand-cut staircase carved into the sandstone.

The pueblo was well-established when Francisco Vasquez de Coronado was the first European to lay eyes on it in 1540. For centuries the Acoma people farmed the valley below the Acoma Pueblo using irrigation canals in the villages closest to the Rio San Jose River.

Sky City was almost destroyed in 1598 when Governor Juan de Oñate, under orders of the King of Spain, invaded New Mexico. The Spanish soldiers began staging raids on Native American pueblos.

In December 1898, a party of Spanish soldiers arrived at Acoma. Initially, they were welcomed and treated in a friendly manner until the soldiers turned aggressive and began to demand grain from the Acoma storehouses.

Acoma dwellings on mesa above sheer-faced cliffs.

The grain was needed by the tribe to survive the winter. The Acoma attacked the soldiers, killing 13 of them, including their commander, Juan de Zaldivar, the nephew of Governor Juan de Oñate.

In response, Oñate resolved to make an example of Acoma. He dispatched 70 of his best men, under the command of Vicente de Zaldivar, to attack the Acoma pueblo.

In 1599, the Spanish troops came into view of the pueblo. The Acoma tribe fanned out from their village to guard the edge of the mesa. As the Spanish drew near, the defenders unleashed a barrage of rocks and arrows on the invaders.

Despite the rocks and arrows, over the next three days the soldiers fought their way to the top. The Spaniards brought small cannon up the back of the mesa and began firing into the village.

The battle then turned into a massacre. When it ended, as many as 800 Acoma people were dead in their ruined pueblo.

Afterwards, the survivors were marched to Santo Domingo Pueblo where all males over the age of 12 were condemned to 20 year's servitude. Of the few dozen Acoma men of fighting age who were still alive after the battle, they were sentenced to have one foot cut off.

The surviving children under the age of 12 were taken from their parents and given to Spanish missionaries to rear. Most of them, including the women, were sold into slavery.

Oñate was tried and convicted of cruelty to Indians and colonists and banished from New Mexico. He appealed the ruling and was cleared of all charges.

The population of Acoma Pueblo was reduced from its population of 2,000 people to some 250 survivors. Some of the Acoma people who had been sold into slavery managed to escape and make their way back home.

A royal decree in 1620 created civil offices in each pueblo, including Acoma. Each office had a governor.

The Acoma people suffered from smallpox epidemics, and raiding from the Apache, Comanche and Ute. On occasion, the Acoma would side with the Spanish to fight against the nomadic tribes.

In later years, the Acoma practiced their religion in secrecy. Intermarriage and intra-racial marriage became common among the Acoma with other pueblos and Hispanic villages.

28

The Vibrator, the Cure for Hysteria

When doctors invented the vibrator two centuries ago, they weren't thinking of sexual pleasure. Today, it is estimated that one-third of adult American women own one.

Until the 20th century, American and European men—including physicians—believed that women did not experience sexual desire or pleasure. They thought that women were simply fleshy receptacles for male lust and that intercourse culminating in male ejaculation fulfilled women's erotic needs.

Women were socialized to believe that "ladies" had no sex drive. Duty required them to put up with sex in order to keep their husbands happy and have children.

This, understandably, left a lot of women sexually frustrated. They complained to doctors of having anxiety, sleeplessness, irritability, nervousness, erotic fantasies, feelings of heaviness in their lower abdomen and wetness between their legs.

This syndrome, in medical terms, became known as "*hysteria*", taken from the Greek for "uterus".

The publication, "Psychology Today", pinpoints the problem of "hysteria". "There are documented complaints of female hysteria that date back to the 13th century. Doctors of that era understood women had libidos and advised them to relieve their sexual frustration with dildos."

In the 16th century, physicians told married "hysterics" to encourage their husbands' lust. Unfortunately, that probably didn't help too much. Modern research shows that only about 25 percent of women experience orgasm consistently from intercourse.

Most women need direct clitoral stimulation, and most intercourse doesn't supply much.

For hysteria unrelieved by husbandly lust, and for widows and single women, doctors advised horseback riding, which for some provided enough clitoral stimulation to trigger orgasm.

In other early cases, doctors and midwives applied vegetable oil to women's genitals and then massaged them with one or two fingers inside and the heel of the hand pressing against the clitoris.

With this type of massage, women had orgasms and experienced sudden, dramatic relief from hysteria. They called them "paroxysms" because everyone knew that women were incapable of sexual feelings, so they could not possibly experience orgasm.

By the early 19th century, physician-assisted paroxysm was firmly entrenched in Europe and the

U.S. The practice proved to be a financial godsend for many doctors.

At the time, the public viewed physicians with tremendous distrust. Medicine was primitive. Most doctors had no scientific training. Their standard treatment, bleeding, killed more people than it helped.

Thanks to genital massage, hysteria was one of the few conditions doctors could treat successfully. It produced large numbers of grateful women who returned faithfully and regularly, eager to pay for another treatment.

For doctors, the treatment of hysteria had a downside. A genital massage resulted in achy, cramped fingers and hands.

In the 19th century, electricity arrived in American homes. The first electric appliances appeared: the electric fan, toaster, tea kettle, and sewing machine.

An enterprising English physician, Dr. Joseph Mortimer Granville, patented the electromechanical vibrator. The vibrator was an immediate hit.

During the 20th century, doctors lost their monopoly on hysteria treatment as women began buying vibrator devices for themselves.

To make vibrators socially acceptable, their real purpose was disguised. They were called personal massagers. A 1903 Sears Roebuck catalog described its popular massager as "a delightful companion—all the pleasures of youth—will throb within you."

29

The Oyster Pirates

Yaquina Bay at Newport, Oregon

Rough and tough ship captains and traders inhabited a settlement at the back of Yaquina Bay known as Oysterville.

A fresh oyster harvest

In the early days, it was a haven for oyster fishermen, as the mollusks were distributed all over the bay. The oysters provided an important food for the Native American tribes that inhabited the area.

Two occurrences became a problem for those depending on Yaquina Bay's oyster crop. The Boston oystermen invaded the area. The demand for oysters grew from a few bushels to a number in infinity.

San Francisco, only a few days sailing from Yaquina Bay, would literally take all the oysters they could get.

The second problem facing Yaquina Bay, was that while the appetite for oysters was unlimited, the supply wasn't.

In 1863, the Siletz Indian Reservation had legal rights to Yaquina Bay and its resources. The Indians contracted with two commercial oystermen—captains Solomon Dodge of the sloop *Fanny* and James J. Winant of the schooner *Annie G. Doyle.*

Dodge and Winant paid the Indians a royalty of $1.15 per bushel of oysters, hauling them directly to San Francisco where they sold them for $10 per bushel.

As the demand for oysters grew, so did the outside interest in Yaquina Bay.

Yaquina Bay's resident oyster pirate was a skipper named Richard Hillyer. He was captain of the schooner *Cordelia Terry*. Hillyer brazenly helped himself to the Indians' oysters.

He claimed it was the free right of all citizens to take fish in American waters. He felt he owed the Indians nothing for the oysters he took.

Some fruitless attempts were made to discuss the issue with Hillyer by the Siletz Indian Agent Ben Simpson. The agent wrote to his supervisor asking for help in enforcing the law.

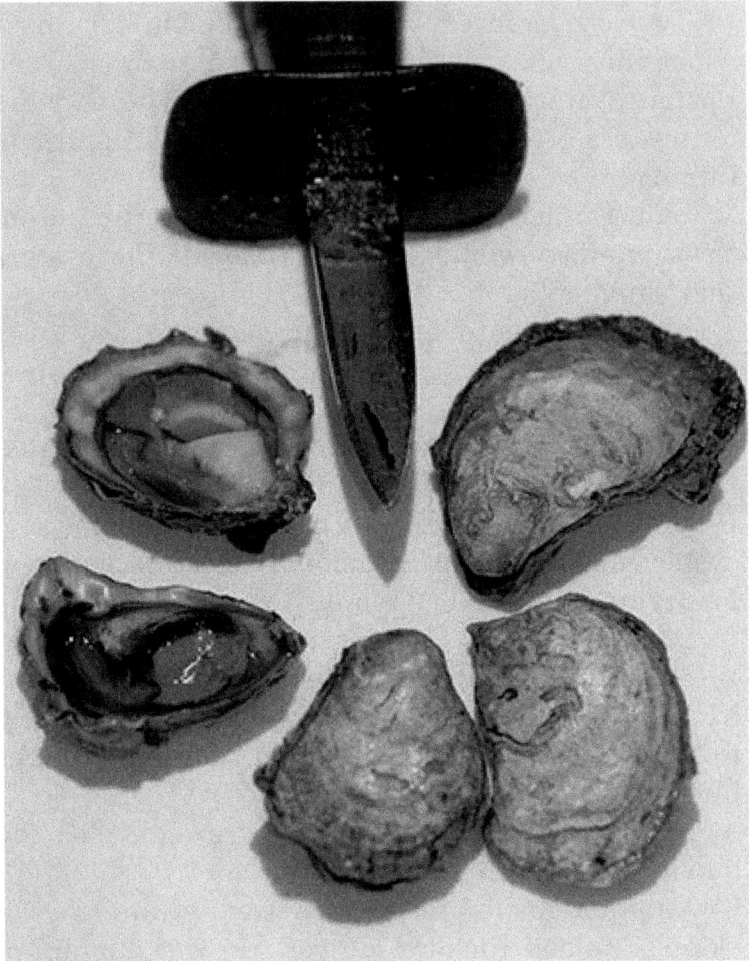

The Olympic variety of oysters.

A small company of U.S. Army soldiers was on its way over the Coast Range from a post on the Yamhill River. The soldiers settled into an encampment near Oysterville.

The soldiers enjoyed a hearty dinner courtesy of the grateful Dodge and Winant. The next day the made a "courtesy" call on Hillyer.

Hillyer received them graciously until they presented him with an injunction to desist from further oyster piracy in Tribal waters. The penalty for neglecting to do so was arrest and prosecution.

Oyster pirate Hillyer agreed to all the terms. The soldiers learned that Hillyer secretly arranged to douse their food that night with enough laudanum to keep them all asleep until noon the following day.

Hillyer's plan was while the soldiers slept off their laudanum-laced meal, to load his boat with oysters and head for San Francisco.

The soldiers, having avoided the doped food the night before, greeted Hillyer early the next morning. Hillyer decided to call the soldiers' bluff. He loaded his ship with oysters and essentially dared them to arrest him.

They borrowed a skiff and rowed out to make the arrest. Hillyer hoisted a British flag, trying to dupe the soldiers into thinking an arrest would cause an international incident.

The soldiers ignored the flag, boarded the ship and arrested Hillyer. They unloaded his ship and hauled him off to Corvallis.

Hillyer filed some lawsuits and criminal complaints, all of which were ignored. He was officially banned from Yaquina Bay. Grudgingly, he returned to his ship and went off to try his luck in the northern fisheries.

In the spring of 1864, Hillyer arrived back at Yaquina Bay. He brought with him a crew of hard-fisted fighters, ready to take what he thought was rightfully his by force.

Agent Simpson against notified the army. This proved to be unnecessary as captains Dodge and Winant had anticipated Hillyer's return. Soon after Hillyer returned, Winant sailed his schooner, the *Annie G. Doyle* into the bay. The Annie G. Doyle was carrying a crew of the roughest, toughest bar fighters on the Central Coast.

A short, but sharp action ensued. When the Central Coast ruffians were through with them, Hillyer's thugs had all they wanted. Hillyer made a full retreat out to sea.

Two years later, Hillyer returned again, running the Cordelia Terry up onto the sand bar. The schooner broke up and sank right beneath Hillyer's feet.

He survived the incident, but left the area and was never heard from again.

30

A Man and His Horse

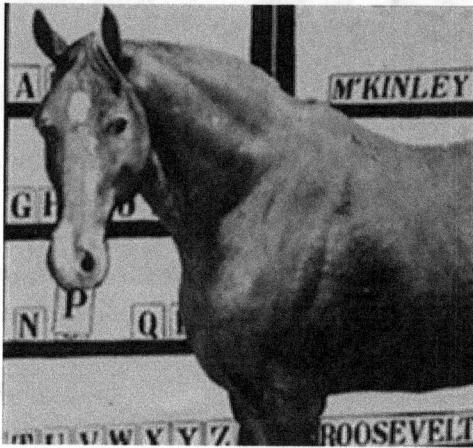

Jim Key, the world's smartest horse.

Illiam "Bill" Key was a former slave, a self-trained veterinarian and a patent medicine salesman. His main talent was training horses.

He was emphatic about the fact that he never used a whip or other cruel techniques to train a horse. Patience and kindness were his only tools, plus an ability to get into a horse's mind.

Dr. Bill Key and his horse, Jim Key.

Bill Key's training accomplishments came through with a horse bearing his own name. The horse was named "Jim Key".

Jim Key could read, write, spell, in political debate. do math, tell time, sort mail, use a cash register and a telephone, He cited Bible passages and engaged in political debate.

The horse became known as the "Marvel" of the Twentieth Century and "The Greatest Crowd Attractant" in America." Jim Key was foaled in 1889 in Shelbyville Tennessee.

He was the offspring of an aging but purebred Arabian mare by the name of "Lauretta Queen of Horses. His sire was Tennessee Volunteer, an illustrious Hambletonian once owned by circus king P.T. Barnum.

The newborn was something of an ugly duckling. Dr. Bill Key didn't expect him to live.

Instead of naming him for a biblical prophet as he had planned, he chose "Jim" after a wobbly local drunk. He kindly gave him his own last name.

Bill Key's slave master died when Bill was five years old. The child was willed to a man named John W. Key, a tanner in Shelbyville, Tennessee. Bill was given the task of keeping his new handicapped master company. The kindly master gave Bill something few slaves received, an education.

His master taught him reading, writing, arithmetic and science. The mistress of the house taught him elocution and etiquette.

When Bill's master died, the family lost their comfortable lifestyle. Bill was well on his way to becoming a success. He stepped in to pay the mortgage and sent the master's sons to Harvard.

When asked about his unusual devotion toward his former master's family, Bill answered, "I was one of those unfortunate men who had a kind master."

During the Civil War, Bill Key worked both sides. He served the Rebels in the battles of Fort Donelson, Stones River and Shiloh. He also served the Yankees by helping fellow slaves flee on the Underground Railroad.

Bill Key was arrested and sentenced to hang as a double-agent. He escaped, thanks to his poker-playing genius. After the war, he went back to Shelbyville, paid off the mortgage on his dead master's fallen property, and supported his master's heirs for the rest of their life.

He established a leading veterinarian practice, a racetrack, hotel, and a restaurant. He made a fortune in the patent medicine business selling Keystone Liniment in his traveling medicine shows.

Dr. Key was 56-years-old when the sickly Jim Key was born. When the foal's dam died, the gangly foal refused to be separated from his owner and trainer.

Jim Key would cause such a ruckus in the barn that Dr. Key was forced to take the colt into his home and out on the road with him to sell Keystone Liniment.

Dr. Key began his serious tutelage of Jim on a whim, thinking he would teach him only one letter of the alphabet, then another, then the rest. Over seven years, he used patience and rewards to teach Jim to read, spell, recognize money, and do basic arithmetic.

In 1897, Dr. Key was asked to serve on the Negro Committee at the Tennessee Centennial Exposition in Nashville. Jim Key came along, making his debut as an educated horse.

President William McKinley declared that Jim Key was the "greatest object lesson of the power of kindness that he ever witnessed".

Press accounts brought more attention. A New York promoter, Albert R. Rogers, offered extravagant sums of money for the horse, Dr. Key declined.

Jim Key performed in expositions, theaters and music halls across the country. He was the top money-maker at the 1904 St. Louis World's Fair, where he performed for then President Teddy Roosevelt's daughter Alice.

When asked to spell Alice's name, he cunningly attached the surname of her escort, Congressman Nicholas Longworth. When the couple was married two years later, Jim Key was declared to be a psychic as well as a genius.

Both the horse and the man were virtually forgotten by the turn of the century.

31

The Lost Colony

Roanoke Island was found abandoned by colonists. Researchers think they now know why.

It was May 8, 1587, when a group of 118 men, women and children left England to sail across the Atlantic Ocean. Under the command of John White, the colonists headed for a destination on the Chesapeake Bay.

The hurricane season was upon them, forcing the colonists to stop their journey earlier than planned. They settled on an island off the North Coast of what is now North Carolina.

The colony on Roanoke Island thus became the first English settlement in the New World. John White's daughter gave birth to the first child of European parents to be born on American soil. Her name was Virginia Dare.

John White was the new governor. He left to return to England to get more supplies. England was at war with Spain and had no ships to spare. It was three years before White could return to Roanoke Island with the supplies.

The Roanoke settlement was stripped of its people. The only trace the colonists left was a mysterious 'cro' carved into a tree and the word "crotoan" carved into a fence post.

Theories differ on why the colonists deserted the island. Some researchers believe their disappearance was due to an annihilating disease. The lost colonists were the third group of English arrivals on North Carolina's Roanoke Island, settling near the modern-day town of Manteo.

The first group came in 1584 to explore and map the land for future groups. A second group came in 1585, charged with a military and scientific mission. Their intentions were farm from peaceful.

That's where tensions began with Native American tribes. The second group was driven out by the Native Indians because the colonists were taking up good land and resources.

The third group came in 1587 with entire families with children. There are differences in the varying reports as to how many men, women and children landed. The number runs from 117 to a high of 150, depending on which source is used.

Researchers are getting closer to learning what happened to the colonists on Roanoke Island when John White left to get new supplies.

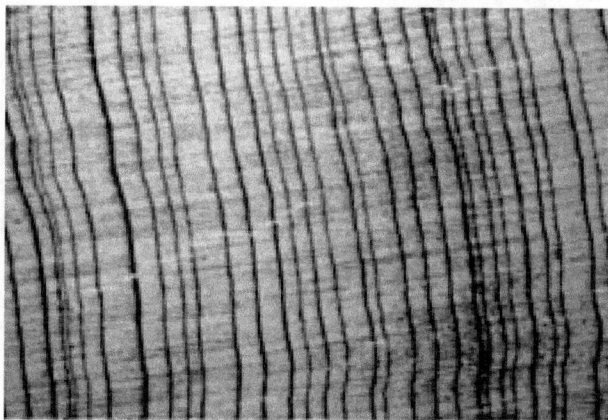

Lost Colony
Drought:
1587-1589

Jamestown
Drought:
1606-1612

Researchers Dennis Blanton, from the College of William and Mary, and climatologist David Stahle, of the tree ring laboratory of the University of Arkansas, sheds some light on the subject.

Blanton and Stahle looked at tree rings along the Blackwater and Nottoway rivers on the Virginia-North Carolina border. Trees grow each year by adding a layer of wood cells. The width of the tree ring indicates how much the tree has grown in a particular growth season.

The rings were smaller than average during the years 1587-1589 and during the years 1606-1612. The tree rings show that the settlement on Roanoke Island coincided with the worst three-year drought of the past 800 years.

"What a time to create a settlement!" exclaimed the authors.

The colonists were expected to live off the land with trade and tribute from the Indians. Because of the drought, neither the colonists nor the Indians had much food to share.

When the Jamestown colonists arrived years later to set up their colony in Virginia, another major drought occurred. Both the Roanoke and Jamestown colonists established settlements during the worst possible times.

There are a number of theories as to what happened to the inhabitants. One theory holds that the people simply left the settlement. It is considered one of the more probable theories.

It is thought they left Roanoke and started settling in Chesapeake Bay. They are believed to have built rafts or a boat, using materials from their houses.

Another theory is the entire population was killed by disease. This theory is discounted because no bodies were found and the houses had disappeared.

A third theory offered is that the village was destroyed by a hurricane. This theory is not considered believable. While a hurricane could have washed away the colonists and destroyed the houses, why was the fence on which they wrote "Crotoan" still standing?

A fourth and more probable theory is the people of Roanoke decided to leave Roanoke to live with the Natives. Crotoan, which was carved on a post, was the name of an island in the area. It was also the name of a group of natives that inhabited it.

A fifth theory is the colonists were killed by the Native Americans. Some consider this the most probable of all the theories put forth.

32

John Wesley Powell
Explores the Grand Canyon

John Wesley Powell

J ohn Wesley Powell prepared well for the three-month trip that would take him and his crew down the Green and Colorado Rivers through the unknown depths of the

Grand Canyon. He began his expedition in Green River City, Wyoming, May 24, 1869.

Powell had four boats especially built for the trip in Chicago. He transported them to the Green River by Union Pacific Railroad.

Three of the boats were made of oak. Each had three separate compartments. The fore and aft compartments were sealed to make them watertight. These sealed compartments were used to stow all of the equipment and provisions needed for the trip.

John Wesley was the son of a Methodist minister who moved his family around a great deal, first to Ohio, then to Wisconsin.

The elder Powell was an avid slavery abolitionist. This stance was so unpopular that young John Wesley was subject to stoning by his classmates. This led to him being home-schooled.

His tutor, a neighbor of the Wesley's named George Crookham, gave John a thorough schooling in the natural sciences. Powell spent all of his spare time exploring the Midwest. He rowed alone along the entire length of the Ohio River.

The 35-year-old Powell became something of an expert on geology and conchology (the study of mollusk shells).

As an impassioned abolitionist, he was one of the first to answer President Lincoln's call for volunteers in the Civil War in 1860. He enlisted as a private with the Twentieth Illinois Regiment. He soon rose to the rank of major, in charge of an artillery battery.

In the Battle of Shiloh, when Powell held up his right hand as a signal for the guns to fire, a Minnie ball struck his wrist. The wounds were severe and the arm had to be amputated at the elbow. He endured surgery for years to ease the pain in the stump.

At the end of the war, Powell's father wrote him. "Wes, you are a maimed man. Settle down to teaching. Get this nonsense of science out of your mind."

Powell contended that his missing arm was not going to stop him from doing whatever he wanted. He did become a geology professor at Illinois Wesleyan University. His wife Emma was about as adventurous as was John. Accompanied by students, they traveled out west.

They traveled by train, wagon and horseback to Denver, Colorado where they climbed Pike's Peak. Powell's wife Emma was the second woman to ever have climbed the majestic mountain. (As a footnote, Pike himself never climbed the peak.)

Powell became obsessed with taking boats down the treacherous white waters of the Colorado River. He was regarded as a serious amateur by some professional scientists. He determined to prove himself.

In 1869, Powell and led an expedition of 10 men in four small boats down the Green and Colorado rivers. He was the first anglo to explore the depths of the Grand Canyon.

In 1871, he won a government grant to map the Colorado Plateau. Powell's subsequent geological descriptions of the region introduced an entire new branch of geology called "geomorphology". This is geology concerned with the structure, origin and development of the topographical features of the earth's surface.

Powell's map of the Colorado

Powell's scientific prestige grew as did his ability to cultivate relationships with important politicians. He was made the second director of the United States Geological Survey in 1881.

He insisted on putting truth before politics, earning him some powerful political enemies. Some western politicians, eager to exploit the natural resources of the West, objected to Powell's insistence on understanding the natural science of a region before developing it. His enemies were able to push Powell out of his post at the United State Geological Survey.

Meet the Author

Alton Pryor has published fifty-plus books since turning 70 in 1997—many of them about California's past and the colorful characters who rode our trails to fame or infamy.

To date he has sold more than 180,000-plus copies of his first book, "Little Known Tales in California History", and has done respectably well with most of his other titles.

But until fate derailed his 33-year journalism career, he never aspired to write a book, and certainly never anticipated he would come to be regarded as "Mr. Self-Publishing" by his peers in the Sacramento area. "I would have liked living in the Old West," he says. "I wanted, at one time, to be a really good cowboy. I had horses as a young man and even took a raw colt and trained it to work cattle."

But, by the time Pryor was born on March 19, 1927, the era of gunslingers and gold miners was over, and he started life, instead, on his family's farm outside of King City in the Salinas Valley.

He was terminated after writing for 27 years for a magazine. The magazine was sold to a midwest firm. Pryor turned to writing books and says now, "I wish I had been fired 20 years earlier."

Index

www.ingramcontent.com/pod-product-compliance
Lightning Source LLC
LaVergne TN
LVHW051458080426
835509LV00017B/1799